The Last Mile

The Last Mile

Broadband and the Next Internet Revolution

Jason Wolf
Natalie Zee

Boston, Massachusetts   Burr Ridge, Illinois
Dubuque, Iowa   Madison, Wisconsin   New York, New York
San Francisco, California   St. Louis, Missouri

McGraw-Hill

A Division of The McGraw-Hill Companies

2 3 4 5 6 7 8 9 BKM BKM 9 0 9 8 7 6 5 4 3 2 1 0

0-07-136349-1

Book design by Michael Mendelsohn at MM Design 2000, Inc.

This publication is designed to provide accurate and authoritative information in regard to the subject matter covered. It is sold with the understanding that neither the author nor the publisher is engaged in rendering legal, accounting, or other professional service. If legal advice or other expert assistance is required, the services of a competent professional person should be sought.

> —From a Declaration of Principles jointly adopted
> by a Committee of the American Bar
> Association and a Committee of Publishers

McGraw-Hill books are available at special quantity discounts to use as premiums and sales promotions, or for use in corporate training programs. For more information, please write to the Director of Special Sales, Professional Publishing, McGraw-Hill, Two Penn Plaza, New York, NY 10121-2298. Or contact your local bookstore.

To my mother Laurie and my wife Rachel.
— *Jason Wolf*

For my parents for their unconditional love and support.
— *Natalie Zee*

Contents

Foreword

I've known Natalie and Jason since their early days at Macromedia. Their individual design talents, coupled with their grasp of the use of technology for creative expression, make them ideal authors of this book. For *The Last Mile: Broadband and the Next Internet Revolution* is not another tome about broadband technology underpinnings; it is a highly readable work that focuses on how broadband will change the landscape.

Even though I am still relatively young (at least that's what I have been telling myself since I recently turned 40), I've been fortunate enough to live through and be involved in an enormous number of computing revolutions. When I started college, I experienced the minicomputer overtaking mainframes. By the time I graduated from Brown and continued there founding a research institute, I got to see the advent of the IBM PC, with its 24 x 80 screens and DOS command-line interface. Soon, bitmapped screens overtook the glass teletypes, and with the advent of Apple's Lisa and Macintosh, as well as Microsoft Windows, the graphical user interface became the preferred means of interaction between human and computer. Workstations from Apollo (I used serial #2) and Sun added networking to allow interaction between people and machines. Later, I joined Macromedia and ran most of its product development from the mid-1990s, and saw the addition of CD-ROMs to every PC, the addition of DVD to PCs, and the commercialization of the ARPANET to become the Internet.

Why do I tell such a long story? Because in their early days, each one of these proposed changes was met with skepticism and doubt by the current technology establishment. "PCs are toys—they'll never be powerful enough." "Bitmapped screens are too expensive—they'll never become mainstream." "Graphical user interfaces use up too much CPU power." However, ultimately, demand by end users for an easy-to-use but rich, compelling multimedia experience caused the revolutionaries to win—and made these "expensive" technologies affordable.

Broadband is happening. I can tell that it's happening because last month 46 million people downloaded Macromedia's Flash player so they could get a better multimedia experience on the Web. I can tell it's happening because Microsoft and RealNetworks report millions of users downloading their audio and video players each month, and tens of millions of page views to listen to and view audio and video on what is largely still a narrowband Internet. I can tell it's happening because people's grandmothers are getting DSL connections.

Broadband is exciting because it will enable the content that people currently consume—on TV, on the Internet, on radio, in movies—to converge. It will enable the creatives out there to express themselves in the way they want, not limited by slow modem connections or textual display formats. It will enable merchants to show their merchandise in a natural form, unconstrained by the limits they have today. It will enable schools to teach through simulation and experimentation, not drill and rote. And most of all, it will enable end users to experience what they want when they want it, without wait.

Broadband is the next revolution. I can tell because I hear the skeptics getting louder. Jason and Natalie's book will show why those skeptics will be wrong, yet again.

Norm Meyrowitz
President of Macromedia

Preface

"Wake up and smell the bandwidth."

Flying cars, talking watches, and robots. Science-fiction movies like *Blade Runner* and *2001: A Space Odyssey* helped us fantasize about a future world where sophisticated technology merged seamlessly into everyday life. But where is technology moving today? More importantly, how can you take advantage of the business opportunities technology is giving us for the future?

Picking up this book is your first step to understanding technology and how it will take us into the imminent future. The broadband revolution will move us further into the realm of science fiction, where a world of technology will become an integral part of our everyday society. First, the typewriter entered the business world, followed by the calculator, and finally the computer. Today, the advancement of business is driven by technological achievements, and in most cases those achievements are funded by businesses. Technology makes the business you are in possible, and the continual advancement of technology will allow all businesses to move quicker, sell more, and offer more to the consumer in the future. Broadband is just one such technology that is here today waiting for businesses to grasp it. The goal of this book is to help you better understand the coming technology and vision ahead—a view just far enough away to energize you with the unlimited possibilities that a broadband world can offer you and your company.

First off, you may be asking questions such as, what is broadband? Why is it such a big deal? How can it help the future of my business? Broadband isn't an idea; it's a technological innovation on the existing copper-based analog phone system that is in place throughout the world today. By altering the analog phone system into a digital one, the consumer who once was told a 56-kbps modem was the speed limit of the Internet is now offered an almost unlimited speed connection. (This is covered in detail in Chapter 2.)

Also, with the introduction of this technological innovation, a race has started between the phone company and the cable companies. The race between these two industries is to see who can get the most number of consumers hooked up with their technology. Because your cable companies and telephone companies are just a few miles from your home, the term *last mile* was coined in reference to this race. This book will help you answer questions, as well as help you figure out the right plan of action your company needs to take. Right now, you may already be successful in the digital economy or have a good understanding of the Internet today and how it works in your business world. But there's a new world approaching that will change how the game is played for the future.

We are writing this book to help you easily understand broadband technically, eliminating all the hype, and to assist you as you plan and adopt your broadband strategy. But in order for you to feel comfortable with us, it's probably a good idea for you to understand where we came from and why we are writing this book. Understand that technology is our passion and we happen to be lucky that it also happens to be a part of our daily job. Running the Research and Development group for marchFIRST (www.marchFIRST.com), a leading global Internet professional services firm that helps companies build visionary business models, brands, systems, and processes, we must constantly keep abreast of new technologies, disseminating important information, creating prototypes, and teaching it to the rest of the company. We know how to weed out the marketing hype because we've seen it and heard it all.

THE BEGINNINGS OF BROADBAND— MACROMEDIA SHOCKWAVE

What started broadband? Certainly many factors influenced the growth of the Internet toward Broadband, but one of the biggest was the porting of an interactive technology from the CD-ROM market to the web browser market. The Macromedia Director playback engine became a plug-in that could be used by Netscape's web browsers, thus unleashing the CD-ROM market onto the Web. As more and more CD-ROM developers gravitated to the Web, more people could view the developers' interactive content.

There was just one problem, however: The Web wasn't even close to being fast enough to support the interactive multimedia experience that CD-ROMs offered. The market didn't seem to care as it just grew and grew. People just continued to develop interactive content for the Web, hoping that some day the speed of the Internet would catch up.

That day has arrived. Behind the scenes, Macromedia has strategically positioned its plug-in for Director into the installer of Navigator and Communicator through a deal with Netscape, making the developer's life easy in terms of distribution. We can specifically remember the exact moment the engineer a few cubes away yelled "It works!" We all went running to his desk to see a very simple interactive Director movie running in a Netscape window. For a good minute, about 10 of us stood there and watched as he scrolled the movie up and down on the page. None of us had any idea what we were really looking at, because at the time, most people had no idea where to even type those funny-looking "http" things. Well, times have certainly changed. Just about everyone has an e-mail address and knows exactly what dot coms are all about.

The next big factor was the introduction of the plug-in version of QuickTime and RealPlayer. These two plug-ins not only allowed video to be played in the browser window but audio as well. Who cared if the movies were the size of a postage stamp and played back at about half a frame per second? Like the Apple IIe that hooked many of us way back when, others were hooked on this new potential too. Video distribution via a computer started a lot of people thinking about other ways of communicating using the computer. About this same time, electronic forms of communication like e-mail, file transferring, and websites were really taking off. Companies started adopting strategies of making the most of the Internet. Businesspeople the world over started seeing the possibilities of interacting with one another, with their customers, and with other businesses electronically. The potential energy that was building was enormous, and that potential was released into a full kinetic fury of a business named Amazon.com. When Amazon effectively demonstrated that a company could not only stand alone by doing business solely on the Internet but could make a monumental fortune at the same time, companies everywhere made a sharp left toward the on-ramp of the information superhighway.

This metaphorical highway was built years ago by our government and was now starting to get really crowded, with thousands of new companies merging on every day. What do you do when the freeways start getting crowded and slow? You build a new, bionic one. Enter broadband.

TRANSFORMING THE WEB INTO AN INTERACTIVE MEDIUM

Now that the Web has video, sounds, text, and graphics and is able to link to other pages using hypertext, interactivity has started to become a buzzword. Interactive websites are all the rage, and trade publications have been making them widely known. Companies everywhere have started to see the bigger picture of the Web's potential. People were really out there, clicking on links, entering their credit cards, and signing up for free e-mail services.

Interacting with the end user became the next logical step. At first, a website was like sending a message in a bottle to your customer. You wrote something, packaged it up, and sent it off—except it cost $10,000 or more. Without advertising your website, which no one did, you had about as much chance of someone finding it as a floating message in a bottle. The hope was someone, from anywhere, would find it, read it, and contact you. But their return contact had to be essentially through another medium, such as a phone or maybe e-mail. There was really no measure of ROI (return on investment) for the effectiveness of a site. Sure, people were talking about "hits per day," making claims like "My company gets 50,000 hits per day." But real web developers knew that you had to first divide all the items on your site by the number of hits to come back with a close approximation of the number of people that were actually doing the clicking. Besides, faking the number of hits was as easy as editing a text file. It meant nothing.

BROADBAND AND THE NEXT INTERNET REVOLUTION

The inspiration for this book was fueled by our passion for technology and its unlimited uses. We are both already accomplished authors working in this highly demanding industry. However, this topic is something we are truly passionate about. We've been talking about broadband so much, to our teams, our peers, and our clients, that it seemed crazy if we didn't spend the extra time to get all of our thoughts on paper to share with the businesses that could really position themselves for the next big Internet wave.

You'll find that we've organized the book into three main parts. Part One is simply "The Broadband Revolution." In this section, we will go though and explain the history of the Internet and mass media, and the current infrastructure for technology. We will also explain in more detail what broadband is, the various ways it can be deployed, the deployment or "last mile" challenges, and the interactive possibilities.

Part Two, "The Impact of Broadband," discusses how the business decisions and mergers from around the globe affect the world and global economy. The section will also talk about how the changing culture of communication, technology, and commerce will affect businesses.

Finally, Part Three, "The Changing Landscape," brings it all back to you. You'll discover how broadband will affect your company and learn the necessary strategies to go from a business-to-business (commonly referred to as B-to-B) focus to a business-to-consumer (B-to-C) one. It also forecasts what life will be like in the future, which helps you better forecast your broadband strategy.

We hope you can take the information in this book and apply it right away in your business. Also, since research is an ongoing process, please visit our website—www.lastmilebook.com—to get timely updates to research and links to some important sites. We are here to help you understand everything you need to know before the last mile is completed.

Jason Wolf
Natalie Zee

Acknowledgments

The first people that I need to thank are my grandparents. They were the ones when I was little who had the answers to questions that ultimately led me to where I am today. Next is my mother. Thanks for staying my mother during the writing of this book, even though I seemed to vanish. I would also like to thank Michelle Reed of McGraw-Hill for being so supportive. Michelle, the book wouldn't have been possible without you. Thanks for not forgetting how big broadband is going to be from our conversations at the restaurant in San Francisco!

And to Andy "let's go skiing" Berry, maybe we could learn to water ski? Finally, to my reason for living, Rachel, there is still no existing technology to measure how much I love you.

And of course to my partner in everything, Natalie Zee, without whom this book "really" would not have been possible, thank you for all the opportunities you have given me thus far in life. And in times of stress don't forget to ask yourself, "If you were a hotdog would you eat yourself?"

Jason Wolf

Thanks to my parents who always encouraged me to do what made me happy. Also, thanks to Professor Howard Besser and the staff at the School of Information Management and Systems at University of California at Berkeley for inspiring and teaching me about the world of new media and technology, to Professor Bar for teaching me about the economics and policies of the Internet, and to Dr. Klee for his excitement and encouragement while I was working on my senior thesis about this new thing called "the Internet." Thanks also to Macromedia, for jumpstarting my career and for continuing to be good to me till this day.

A big thank you to Michelle Reed, a great editor and friend, who has been instrumental in my book-writing career. Thanks also go to all my friends and colleagues who would send me research, quotes, anything related to broadband because they knew I was working on this book, specifically, Matt Connors, Daniel Jenett, George Arriola, and Olivia Warnecke. I also want to thank all the case studies developers for taking time out of their busy days to answer questions. Thanks also to my roommates, Maggie and Dani, who helped feed me and kept me laughing when I really needed a good laugh. I also can't forget my favorite actress, Karen Vigna, who has always supported me in my endeavors. Most of all, thanks to Jason Wolf, my dear friend whom I look up to. I am indeed very lucky to have you as my partner in crime.

Natalie Zee

PART ONE

The Broadband Revolution

CHAPTER 1

Building the Foundation for Broadband

A Look to the Future and a Look at the Past

In the early 1990s, consumers were regaled with the promise of more than 500 television channels and "universal access." Bill Clinton and Al Gore spoke of the "Information Superhighway" as something that was going to become a national and world treasure, and a world in which the Internet would completely revolutionize the way in which consumers and businesses live, work, and interact with each other. We were gonna be wired, we were gonna be empowered, and we were gonna like it!

Much like something out of a John Ford Western, or perhaps more accurately, out of a science-fiction fantasy such as *Blade Runner*, sometimes we, as professionals either working directly in or around this new Internet industry, feel more like pioneers, going against the status quo, venturing forth into uncharted territory, and forging new ground in order to stake our claim on the Internet. When the Internet came to the attention of the general public in the early 1990s, it was greeted with both accolades and skepticism. The few people who did embrace it in the early days really understood the value it brought in terms of community, communications, and its noncommercial nature at the time. For the most part, it was said to be a fad. Journalists would further spawn skepticism with sensationalism, writing articles that focused on cyberhackers or pedophiles and choosing to focus on the dangerous back alley of the Internet.

Remember e-commerce when it first came on the scene? Everyone thought it wouldn't be successful. The technology wasn't there yet; therefore, the pundits said that the consumer market wouldn't embrace e-commerce. Mass media reported on the fears the public would have of buying tangible goods online and the issues of security with credit card fraud. Other brick and mortar stores claimed how ridiculous it would be for them to have an online store when they were doing perfectly fine with their physical stores.

But back then, little-known Amazon.com thought differently. It created an online store selling books from around the world. Customers in small towns from Maine to Mississippi suddenly had the world's bookstore at their fingertips. True, Amazon.com didn't make money its first year, but now it has grown into a monolithic brand leader in the Internet e-commerce industry, selling not only books, but toys, electronics, music, and a lot more. As an early adopter in the e-commerce realm, Amazon.com has helped push traditional bookstores such as Barnes & Noble and Borders to follow suit with online book-stores as well. Because so many of these big name brands are starting to create online stores, we will see a shake up—with smaller companies selling specialized goods because they may not have the advertising dollars to promote their sites. Whatever the case, you can be sure that e-commerce is here to stay.

Presently, broadband is the focus of the moment and the promise of the future. It is projected that by the year 2002, upward of 16 million users in the United States will be connected to the Internet via broadband. The naysayers claim that this projection is not going to happen because not everyone has access to a computer. In reality, technology is developing new ways to transfer information. The majority of people in the United States have TV sets connected to cable lines and cell phones in their pockets. It's time to think of broadband in relation to the future and the way in which life will be more seamlessly integrated with technology. Computer chips are cheap now. Everything in your house will have a computer chip. You can even purchase a $4.99 children's book (with traditional "pages" that turn) that has a computer chip in it.

Projected Broadband Growth

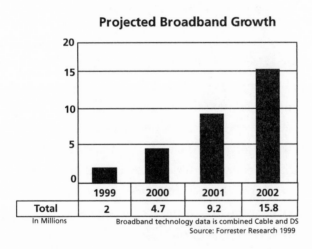

	1999	2000	2001	2002
Total	2	4.7	9.2	15.8

In Millions   Broadband technology data is combined Cable and DS
Source: Forrester Research 1999

Broadband is the next revolution on the horizon, and the same learning curve and lessons of dismissal in the past should be applied. Technology news is making front-page headlines in such highly respected traditional media sources as *The New York Times* and *The Wall Street Journal.* CEOs such as Bill Gates and Steve Jobs aren't only running top technology companies, they are celebrities as well. A two-hour cable TV movie was based on their lives. Technology and the Internet are not only creating a new industry but a new culture as well. Lately, the mass media have responded to the challenge by doing a better job of trying to educate the business world, the public, and themselves on topics that change as fast as the weather. But who are their sources? Where is their information coming from?

Through analysis of media hype and new technology (we promise we will be gentle here), and discussions on the history of the Internet and the changing role of mass media, we hope to show how the progression and convergence to broadband will benefit you in the evolution of your business. You won't be planning a simple road; you'll be planning a highway.

THE POWER OF 2000

As contrived as it may sound, the symbolic nature of the new millennium helps remind us that we have arrived at the future. Just knowing that we are now living in the year 2000 positions each of us in a better state mentally to take a bird's-eye view of where we might be headed and the direction we want to take.

Yet if we are already here in the future, why are we involved in endless debates over policies, deployment issues, media mergers, and dot com hype? If you think about progression and evolution, most developments take time. As the saying goes, Rome wasn't built in a day. However, in our fast-paced society, we want everything now, this very second. Some people are in a mad rush to spew out generalized comments to try and debunk ideas that go against the status quo simply because they don't really understand it. No one really takes the time to think through and ask why we are doing this, how we can do it right, and at what cost/benefit is the venture in terms of profits and social responsibility to the next generation. Everyone is just following everyone else. It's time to take the advice of Apple and "Think Different"—or rather, in this case, "Think Ahead"—and start planning early to build a strong and good foundation for the broadband revolution.

Today consumers can surf the endless supply of hundreds of channels on digital cable; get calls, pages, and e-mail messages on their cell phones; order DVD movies from such websites as Kosmo; and get their groceries delivered to their homes from sites like Webvan. So we're there already, right? Actually, almost. In the course of the last five years, the Internet has sustained most of its hype, proving that the technology has longevity. What we will start to see in the coming century is the seamless adaptation and integration of technology into our lives.

THE LEARNING CYCLE

Before we begin, let us describe the learning cycle framework that has worked so well for companies such as McKesson, Hewlett-Packard, Bank of America, and Levi Strauss & Co. The learning cycle for any project goes through three stages. The first stage is the *automation* phase—the basic phase where information is gathered to make the process faster and more efficient. This information is then tested to support new functions in the *experimental* phase. The end result of the two phases is the *reconfiguration* phase, where the successful experiments are redeployed into the automation phase. When Levi's first introduced custom-made jeans in 1995 with its "Personal Pair" line, the jeans were available only to women. A salesclerk at a department store had to take the customer's measurements, record them, and enter the information into the computer to send it off to the factory. Through its research and the successful introduction of the product, Levi's has since then expanded that first line into the present "Original Spin" line, which gives both men and women the opportunity to have custom-made jeans or khakis. And using new technology, it offers high-tech body scans in its flagship San Francisco store to obtain accurate body measurements.

In the business world, you'll always want to be ahead of the competition as well as to adapt to the changing tides of technology. This cycle is one that runs constantly, always building a better process and product. It is in this manner that the learning cycle can be applied, with its moving circular trajectory, to always make sure that we are keeping up to par with what's relevant for today and what's necessary to lead for tomorrow.

HUMBLE BEGINNINGS

The digital technology of the Internet—that is, the transformation from one-way analog conduits to futuristic fiber-optics lines—will lay the path for what will determine how we communicate, work, and live in society. Unlike the analog world, the digital medium knows what information it is transmitting. Information is treated as digital bits, a formation of 0s and 1s. These bits in the broadband world will travel down high-capacity fiber-optic cables, replacing outdated copper wires, or perhaps even cables will be obsolete as data transmits over wireless networks. The future implementation of these technological factors will determine how consumers receive broadband applications and how we as business leaders can better target them. These concepts of broadband can already be put into action today.

As you no doubt know, the Internet is a vast computer network that links computers all over the globe. It has become the prototype of the future network, giving us a glimpse of what may lie on the horizon as digital technology meshes into our daily lives. Starting back in the late 1950s with the Russian launch of Sputnik, American President Dwight D. Eisenhower saw a need for a group focused on developing strategies for advanced technologies—a specialized Research and Development group. The Advanced Research Projects Agency, ARPA, was then formed as a part of the U.S. Department of Defense. After launching the

United States' first successful satellite, ARPA refocused its efforts to computer networking and communications technology. Looking to make computers more interactive, ARPA broadened its sector to include academics and researchers at leading universities. Thus, ARPANET was formed, and the beginning of the Internet as we know today was born from that first computer network. Of course, we can't forget how innovations from people such as Tim Berners-Lee (hypertext) and Marc Andreessen (Mosaic browser) further revolutionized the Internet technology from ARPANET and pushed it even further with the creation of the World Wide Web.

What's important to note is that back then ARPANET was a collaborative effort in order to create a means of communications through computer networks. That key concept is something often forgotten in the rush to get ahead. It's important to keep in mind, as the Internet becomes the foundation for growth with broadband, that we need to be in touch with not just the technology but also our users/customers, because they are the ones who will help define how the technology is used.

POLICIES FROM THE PAST FOR THE FUTURE?

The National Information Infrastructure (NII) began much of the hoopla when it was heavily touted by the Clinton administration in late 1993. The Clinton administration hoped to create a new method by which the United States could profit and achieve a broad range of economic and social goals. The idea is that all citizens can be connected to a network where they can easily obtain information, exhibit their ideas, and communicate freely. The Internet is estimated to be used by more than 349 million people around the world who use the network to send and receive e-mail, discuss important (or not so important) issues, and travel around the world for information, all from their personal computer. E-commerce has also fueled that growth and adoption of the Internet not simply as a place to amuse oneself, but to run a business as well.

Vice President Al Gore proposed in the late 1990s to remove regulating roadblocks to promote competition. Gore's hopes lay in the fact that this would enable what he believed to be the core of what the NII should represent—equal and wide access to information. One NII policy document states, "Because information means empowerment, the government has a duty to ensure that all Americans have access to the resources of the Information Age." Of course, it is difficult to imagine that everyone will have access at first. There is a significant economy of scale when it comes to technology. Nonetheless, the government seeks to implement changes in the policy matters because private-sector corporations, for example, Microsoft, AT&T, and Time Warner/AOL, are the ones that are developing and starting the basis of the infrastructure. It is impossible to predict, however, how democratic the Internet will be because of the problems with universal access. Universal access is in hot debate because it is said that the early adopters to technology will have an unfair advantage over those who aren't in areas that are wired or technologically advanced because of social or economic reasons. Also, e-commerce has brought on a number of issues as well with regard to taxation. Since some online stores have no physical presence, which state receives the taxes? Is it justifiable to not charge taxes or to have each state resident pay his or her respective state tax? Sounds confusing, doesn't it?

As we advance forward toward the new Information Age, new reforms need to be in place. Many of the previous regulatory laws were enforced under a completely different time period, the Industrial Era. As time marches on, business and technology professionals in this industry are faced with current problems that use old solutions to solve them. As the debate goes on about policy plans, many are fearful that technology will be shaped more along the lines of broadcasting or cable TV structures. Many experts believe that the First Amendment rule of print medium suffices better. Who's right?

Most of this debate is created to relieve the pressure on Congress to bring about timely measures that will enhance the Clinton administration's vision of the NII. But the reality is that most senators and representatives are too limited in technological experience and real know-how to come to any quick significant conclusions. Besides, they keep referring to old models of previous industries that don't apply when it comes to the Internet.

Case in point: the scrutiny at present over Microsoft's position as a monopoly because of its dominance in the industry with both its operating software and its bevy of software applications and Internet browsers. The government believes that Microsoft has an unfair advantage over others because it owns the majority of the operating systems out there, thereby controlling what browsers and software people ultimately use on their machine. A recommendation by the government is in place for Microsoft to split itself into two separate companies, one that handles the computer operating systems and another that handles software and web browsers. As chairman, Bill Gates would have to choose which company he wants to head because it's possible the government will only allow him to hold stock in one or the other. But is Microsoft really a monopoly? Will people be able to get on the Internet as easily on a brand-new PC with no preinstalled web browser?

It's being compared to the great showdown in the 1980s with AT&T and its ultimate breakdown into eight "baby bells." However, many are not sure that the regulatory issue with Microsoft is quite the same. AT&T was clearly running a monopoly because users had no choice in long distance—period. You couldn't just whip up your own long-distance company out of thin air and chose to go with them. But in Microsoft's case, any user could bypass Microsoft Internet Explorer either by downloading the free Netscape browser or by choosing to use an Apple computer running an Apple OS and using Netscape browsers for the Internet. There is no forced nature of usage. People do have a choice in this industry. With so many Internet- and technology-related companies booming in revenue, it could be a misleading warning sign to government officials that the Internet economy will take on the same towering nature as occurred previously with leaders of the Industrial Era.

Microsoft continues to dispute the charges, and the case will be in courts for the next few years. The outcome will be terribly important to everyone, as it indicates what kinds of decisions and policies will be made for technology's future.

E-COMMERCE EMERGENCE

As e-commerce becomes one of the standard ways to mark your digital space online, its introduction to the Internet world was generally not fully accepted until just a short two years ago. It became difficult to justify the costs to bring a digital store to fruition. Plus, the medium is so new that the business success models are still in the process of ironing out details. The media claims that in the next two years we'll see a growth of e-commerce stores shutting down, but isn't that the reality of any business in the world of competition? Retail stores in the physical world have just as hard a time succeeding. How do you make sure your online shop is the one that sustains the hype and becomes a destination?

Amazon.com broke through and did something different, despite the initial skeptics saying that CEO Jeff Bezos was crazy. Perhaps, "crazy" in this industry should mean "innovative," because every innovator from Einstein to Edison was said to be crazy. Amazon.com didn't just sell books; it allowed readers to comment on books and rate them, bringing community along with e-commerce. Using the power of the Internet as a communications medium, Amazon.com differentiated itself from brick and mortar bookstores because the posting of comments became an indirect way to allow potential readers (and customers) to decide whether or not they wanted to purchase the book. Of course, later, Amazon.com got in a bit of trouble when it was leaked out that publishers had the opportunity to pay for special editorial sections of the site in order to promote new books. These books got preferential treatment and were either showcased on main pages or were dubbed an "Amazon.com Pick." Nonetheless, Amazon.com is a good example of a company helping to define commerce in our digital future.

Similarly, other websites, such as Nike.com, tie in special-interest stories on athletes or special marketing sites on sporting events to create an overall online destination, rather than simply an online store. Nike uses these stories and events to create a loyal customer base that will return to the site for content and also information on new products, where a subsequent purchase can happen either online or in their retail space.

These days, the evolution of e-commerce has allowed for more creative ways to engage consumers. In turn, more creative marketing and advertising know-how from agencies and business are needed. The traditional models don't seem to apply anymore in an age where anything goes.

MASS MEDIA CONVERGENCE

Before the onset of television and cable, radio dominated the home as the major source for information from news to entertainment. With the onset of television in the 1950s, did radio die? No, but its focus changed and shifted. Both television and radio have found a balance in terms of behavior and usage. Radio allows for more of a two-way communication between the station and the user. Most people feel comfortable enough to call in to their local radio station to comment on issues on talk radio or to ask a DJ to play a particular song. Television takes a different form of entertainment, allowing users to sit back and be entertained, sending a one-way form of communication.

The Internet is becoming a hybrid of all mass media models. One is not going to replace the other. Rather, a sort of natural selection is taking place, where the best qualities and attributes can be combined to create a medium that is effective in constantly improving the mass communication foundation. With broadband coming on the scene, many are concerned that computers will turn into TVs and TVs will be computers. Does that really matter? Technology is providing businesses and consumers with more options. Whether you want to listen to radio station 104.5 on the radio or on the Web is up to you. If you want to watch your DVD on your TV's DVD player or on your laptop is also your call. It all depends on the situation.

Looking back at the history of mass media when TV came on the scene and people claimed it was the end of the film industry is quite amusing. The film industry is still going strong, as is the television industry. In a similar manner, a balance between mass media models will happen, and for the most part, there will simply be more options to choose from.

MEDIA AND INTERNET MERGERS

In the technological background, as information is increasingly growing, new developments in the architecture itself is garnering much support from the media industry giants. Already because of the Internet, developments have been made in packet switching, whereby information is delivered in chunks of bits and routed separately in order to eliminate traffic. More importantly, this has started the distribution of digital goods. Many companies see this as an opportunity to expand. Musicians are finding new venues for their music. Independent filmmakers are excited about producing their own online content. But Hollywood still wants you to pay attention to them.

Entertainment studios such as Miramax and Sony are partnering up with Internet companies such as SmartSound.com and TowerRecords.com, in alliances that would allow for downloadable digital music, movies as video-on-demand, and projects that are pure web content. These companies hope these advances will lead to big profit for studios that want a piece of the money. Also, as there are no real hard-and-fast rules in the new digital economy, the old studio structure can be shaken up and more freedom can ensue.

Hence, many studios and agencies are spinning off their own little Internet companies, hoping not only to venture into new ground but also for the financial success of an IPO. There becomes an increased blurring of companies. Mergers between previously unlikely subjects such as telephone companies, cable companies, and entertainment studios are all vying for a piece of the future.

Try this for size. Viacom merged with Blockbuster. Then, Paramount merged with Viacom. Now, Viacom has merged again with CBS. All this happened in the course of six years. Having "mass media" (here a cable company, top movie-rental store, movie studio, and one of the Big Three television networks) all under one roof will allow for the company to tap into the specialties of each individual company and use this as they merge into a broadband company. MTV bought sonicnet.com and spun off its interactive division as MTVi (the i is for interactive). NBC bought the web portal snap.com and then spun off a site as NBCi. Both

MTVi and NBCi are creating online presences that currently support the television counterparts, eventually in the broadband world, merging seamlessly between the two with content services that will continue their brand recognition into this new era. MTVi hopes that it becomes the music destination, and NBC wants to continue to be the primary source of news and entertainment.

These cross-pollinating hybrid corporations are finding that their mixed blessings are creating more havoc on their respective specialties. Everyone's following everyone else—with no clear-cut direction or understanding of the nature of the Internet, except its financial viability. There has been a movement toward building bridges and ties that can broaden a corporation's horizon. The only trouble with that is no one can see where the world of technology is really headed. The media hoopla about technology has made industry giants excited and hasty in their mad rush to define the new media. Local telephone companies are waiting to provide cable TV service, and television broadcasters want to use their airwaves for new communication services rather than simply TV. This merging/blurring among communications giants is changing the definition and hierarchy of the media elite.

As the distant rings of the "golden age" of AT&T are just about to fall from our memory, local monopolies are being challenged to survive. Local telephone companies like Pacific Bell in California are now providing high-speed DSL service. They are fearful that the rise of cellular phone usage will diminish their profits. Some are even veering off into the long-distance service market. On the other side of the story, the possibility of booming business in direct-satellite TV (also video-on-demand), which brings crisp digital quality to the TV screen, will give substantial competition to the cable and broadcast TV industries alike. This explains why TV broadcasters are looking into other ventures for their national airwaves. Think about the cable news network MSNBC, a joint venture by Microsoft and NBC with online and broadcast cable news.

The mergers are creating headlines, but for most of them, their actions have yet to be seen. However, it is the sheer excitement over these unions that is creating mass confusion within the industry. Corporations are worried over their future and their upcoming role in the digital age. Hence, they are rushing into each other, merging with each other in the hopes of gaining our attention. And they have, only in the form of fleeting media spectacles.

DEATH OF THE COUCH POTATO?

Many of the mergers between communication giants rest on the hopes of the future of television. Why? Because for the most part, more people have TVs than computers in their homes and the television industry has already become established with its array of television and media studios such as NBC, ABC, and CBS and cable networks such as CNN, TNT, and ESPN. No longer are consumers restless couch potatoes; in the world of digital media, televisions are transformed into interactive agents with set-top boxes that are more powerful than any PC.

Interactive television is the merger of basic television with the intelligence of the computer, and a connection to the Internet. The trend here is that interactive TV will be a hybrid of television and the Web. Currently this hybrid will happen with set-top boxes, and later on these computer technologies will be integrated directly into television. Therefore, consumers will be able to watch what they want, when they want, and at the same time, companies like yours will be able to target your customers directly, knowing instantly whether they like or dislike a product, and allowing them a medium to directly buy your goods or services. Advertising models will change because the focus will be directing customers to an instant buy, instead of traditional TV advertising of today. With plenty of deals in the works to transform the world of television, such as the Viacom/CBS agreement, cable modem services like Excite@Home, and set-top product boxes such as ReplayTV and TiVO, consumer choice will be the ultimate factor in how interactive TV will evolve.

NEXT STEPS

In order for us to progress smartly into the broadband era, we need to create a new paradigm that is redefined, not repackaged. In the rush of corporate mergers, media giants are overly worried about the possible displacement of their industry. The rush of electronic publishing, interactive television, and media hype is holding most of the professional world back from seeing the big picture. Radio and movies still exist, even though it was determined that the advent of television would replace them. To think that digital technology will wipe out these existing media is too quick and hasty a prediction. Electronic publishing and interactive publications may find that some users prefer their print counterpart. However, they may also discover that broadband video and electronic publications are useful to a different niche group.

It is this rush to compete and grab a market we know little about that is creating an atmosphere of chaos. When all of the media hype has settled, there will be a new way of thinking about broadband. The Internet is another alternative and need not be a replacement for everything. Users and consumers will be the final players who will shape the use of these new technologies. Mass media and their convergence with technology will increasingly affect our lives more than we think in the next century. The present model of the Internet will be under significant construction as the NII begins to take form. The learning cycle may work well for corporations to create efficiency, but corporations do not reflect on the nature of society. Our biggest problem with implementing this type of technology is to get access for a broader span of the population and still contain the specialized/personalized content the Internet seems to exhibit. What will happen when commercialization begins to dominate the network? To get more usage, will we revert back to the "lowest common denominator" factor that is so frequently used? People may be relegated to using this technology as nothing more than yet another form of entertainment.

The paradigm is slowly shifting, and we are finding ourselves at the brink of what constitutes the digital world. Each of us is posed with an opportunity to help shape our digital economy.

CHAPTER 2

What Is Broadband?

If you are the type of person who generally skips the technical section of books, don't do that here. Even if your VCR is still blinking "12:00," we're confident that you will be able to understand the technology involved as described in this chapter. The word *broadband* is the hybrid of two words: *broad* and *bandwidth*. But what exactly is bandwidth? When you access the Internet, you are connected via a copper wire such as a phone cord or Ethernet cable. These wires transmit electrical information in much the same fashion that a water pipe provides water to your kitchen sink. (But, please, don't go out and connect your garden hose to your PowerBook.) Now, if you asked your plumber to increase the amount of water that your kitchen can receive because you plan to install a dishwasher, you might hear the plumber say "I'll have to install a thicker pipe." Thicker equals broader, and the size of the "pipe" is what determines the amount of bandwidth it can handle. A small, narrow pipe has very limited bandwidth and a wide one has the potential for high bandwidth. In terms of copper wires, such as phone lines and Ethernet cables, it's the thickness that determines the bandwidth.

Simply put, if you had thicker copper wires connecting you to the Internet, you would have a faster, broader connection. This means broadband is the increase of bandwidth to you and your customers. Technically, something is *broadband-capable* when it can transmit more than 1.5 Mb (megabits) of data per second, but don't worry about that now.

If all this bandwidth and copper talk has you thinking "Who cares?" at this point, think about it like this: All that copper is the foundation of the Internet, and without it your business could not grow. Right now the industry is built on a copper foundation that is too small to support the growth rate. So, many different groups are trying to solve this problem by either building on the existing foundation (such as ADSL, for asymmetric digital subscriber line) or abandoning it and building a new one with wild, some might even say alien, technology (such as fiber optics).

The important thing to realize is that you have time to make some decisions and start planning for this now. Start now, however, because, as someone once said, doing nothing in business is the same as falling behind. Broadband technologies are here today, ready to be rolled out, but it will take some time before, for example, you can count on your mom having a sufficiently high speed connection to the Internet for you to push video her way. There are a lot of competing technology players that believe they have the solution that you should pay attention to, but no standards have emerged as of yet. This lack of standards means you need to familiarize yourself with what is currently out there and on the horizon. Computer manufacturers are already saying that by Christmas 2000, they will be shipping PCs with internal cable and/or DSL modems preinstalled. When this happens, it will cause a giant surge in the number of broadband subscribers. Current estimates indicate about 10,000 people per day are signing up for some type of broadband provider, and that number is only going to go up. Once you understand the playing field, you can start making decisions about the direction you and your company should take.

The simple thing to remember about all the broadband technologies is that they are all much faster connections, in some cases 50 or 100 times faster than old modems. And on top of the speed, they are "always on," that is, always connected, just like a work environment. This is your big advantage. Because of its importance, let me say it another way: Taking advantage of the fact that your customer is going to have an always-on connection is more important than trying to take advantage of their high-speed abilities. The features and functions that your site provides to consumers are far more important than the amount of data you try to cram their way.

COMPETING TECHNOLOGIES

Many different communication industries realized that the Internet wasn't a passing fancy and started serious investigations into new delivery technologies. The first major innovation that all communication providers made was the *digitizing* of the signal. An audio cassette tape is analog, and a CD is digital. You'll notice that you don't see many cassette tapes around any more. If you remember, the digital-to-analog conversion also started all the "500 channels of cable" talk a while back. Well, the same digital conversion technology is being applied to the way we connect to the Internet, thus creating the broadband revolution. But what technology will customers be attracted to? What do you need to develop for a DSL user or a cable modem user? Frankly, it doesn't matter what technology your customer chooses. Regardless of your customers getting a DSL, cable modem, wireless, or satellite connection, you can count on two things: (1) increased bandwidth (read: faster connection) for all of them and (2) for DSL and cable, a persistent connection. Let's talk briefly about the involved technologies before going into their potential uses.

ADSL, VDSL (very high rate digital subscriber line), cable

modems, and fiber optics are just some of the technology terms that you might have heard tossed around lately. (If you haven't, and your business relies on the Internet, it's a good thing you picked up this book.) There are so many broadband access technologies out there that it might make you a bit dizzy. Bear with us because we think it's important that you at least hear them all and recognize what is involved. The technologies include ATM (Asynchronous Transfer Mode) networking, ADSL and VDSL modems, cable modems, fiber optics, wireless access, and electrical power line distribution. Once you are comfortable understanding how each one "gets to the customer," you should be able to see the potential that your company has in reaching your new broadband customers.

We also want to make it clear here that the above-mentioned technologies are competing indirectly (and in some cases very directly) against one another for consumer market share. If the consumer adopts one broadband technology over another (for example, DSL), the DSL providers could become sole providers of consumer Internet distribution. We don't believe that one specific technology is going to emerge the winner in the broadband space, leaving the others abandoned. However, we do believe that one technology is going to get around 50 to 75 percent of the consumer market and all the others will be split among that remaining 25 percent. Presently, the current leader is the cable modem, with DSL in second place.

ATM

ATM is the first acronym you will run across, and, sorry, it doesn't stand for "automatic teller machine." ATM, or asynchronous transfer mode technology, concerns the way your data is sent via the Internet in a broadband environment. ATM is not really the communication method that major companies use. Rather, the focus here is on broadband networks for consumers and how that is going to impact your business. ATM network technology was designed with broadband in mind from day one. It's important that computers agree on how data is sent and received; otherwise, your e-mails, files, and websites originating from a San Francisco computer might not make it out of the city, much less to New York or Europe.

With ATM networks, data is sent in chunks, 53 bytes at a time. Think of a "byte" as one letter or number. Then string a bunch of those chunks together, and you get words, sentences, books, sounds, video, and so on. Without the standard of ATM in place, building broadband infrastructures just wouldn't be practical. Now, this isn't a competing technology but is rather the way the soon-to-be-mentioned technologies work. It's a necessary foundation to be aware of when learning about broadband.

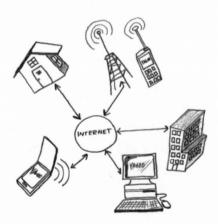

Let's contrast a broadband ATM network with the network infrastructure that is in place at a typical major corporation. Big companies have a highly effective but rather "consumer-ineffi-cient" networking architecture. Because the general consumer needs to download (receive) more data than upload (send) and usually does it at random intervals, ATM technology used by DSL, for example, is perfectly designed to meet these needs. The typical high Internet traffic office has to take the needs of hundreds or thousands of people into consideration. Corporations larger than 500 people are generally connected to the Internet via a fiber-optic backbone that can handle more data per second than the average home user uses per year. Not to mention that connections like this cost thousands per month. Ask your IT manager sometime if your company uses fiber optics. IT managers are also a good resource for understanding how to build an e-commerce network, because it's usually no different than a large office network.

Because the Internet needs of the home user and corporate user are different in terms of technology but not in terms of "bandwidth" requirements, different companies started coming up with home versions of high-speed connections to complete the last mile. Some fairly fast connections are now readily available to consumers that already have plain old telephone or cable TV in the form of DSL and cable modems. When these technologies start rolling out more and more, the consumer is going to start choosing sites (companies) that offer more compelling interactions over the more mundane ones.

ADSL AND VDSL

ADSL (again, the acronym stands for asymmetric digital subscriber line) gives your customers the ability to connect to a website with an effective throughput around the 150 kbps range. If you've ever experienced a 56-kbps modem, where the effective throughput is about 3 kbps, DSL is not only smoking fast, but you can never go back. For example, downloading a 10-MB file is a matter of a few seconds, whereas a 56-kbps connection could tie up your phone line until Christmas. In most cases, your home connection can feel faster than the one at work. DSL is a major competitor in the field of players, thus making phone companies and DSL service providers the ones to watch. We'll talk in depth about this after an overview of all the competitors.

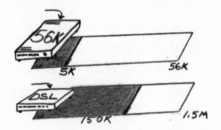

There is an additional subset of DSL technology known as VDSL, which, again, stands for "very high speed DSL." This type of service is similar to the ADSL technology but can handle around 50 MB of data per second. However, in general, you don't need to take this type of connection into consideration, because it is generally out of the scope of the average consumers needs and way out of their price range.

CABLE MODEMS

In this corner, we have the current heavyweight champion of broadband technologies—the cable modem. A cable modem is nothing more than a modified cable box that allows your computer to be hooked to it. Then, the Internet is sent to your computer through your cable line, and your cable box is the "splitter" that decides what goes to your computer and what goes to your TV.

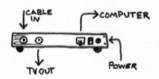

Cable modems do have a few drawbacks, however, including the difficulty of wiring two devices (the television and the computer) that are often are in separate rooms some distance from one another. In addition, there are certain privacy issues with cable modems that you might find unacceptable. Since your entire neighborhood shares a connection to the same cable line, your neighbor could gain access to your computer files and printer. On the other hand, cable modems are fast and cheap, and people can readily understand the advantages of having one.

Cable modems work much in the same way DSL works. The amount of data that can travel via an analog copper line is far less than a digital signal being sent down the same line. This conversion from analog to digital is where cable companies and phone companies discovered this hidden bandwidth. That discovery is putting DSL and cable modems head to head against each other. This is good because it drives the price of high-speed Internet access for the consumer down.

FIBER OPTICS

Practically everyone has heard the term *fiber optics* before, but few truly know what these little miracles are all about. Fiber optics will someday soon replace all the copper wire used for data communication in the world—everywhere. We're not talking about "electrical lines" (where you plug in your vacuum), but phone lines, computer cables, cable TV lines, Internet communication, and so on. Before fiber optics, the only means of data communication was electrical. This was done by either copper wires or electromagnetic (radio) waves broadcast through the air. Fiber optics offered up a secondary solution to communication distribution. Instead of electrical transmission, fiber optics uses pluses of light. Generally, the light is coherent laser light that offers almost unlimited bandwidth. When fiber entered the scene, it made a serious impact in the data distribution market. After all, fiber optics can be about half as thick as your mouse cable but can carry 100 million times more data than an equivalent copper telephone line. For obvious reasons, all major data transmission companies now use fiber optics.

Because of the enormous bandwidth fiber offers, one single cable run to your house will allow your computer, phone, TV, and interactive devices all simultaneous access to the Internet and its resources. There is no end to the bandwidth possibilities. So, if fiber is the future, why doesn't everyone have it? Good question! They will; it's only a matter of time. The trouble is, companies that currently provide data transmission have billions of dollars invested in the copper wires that are strung from their central offices to our homes. This investment is bogging down the growth rate of the inevitable coming new Internet age. Not to mention that fiber is more expensive per pound than copper, and splicing together two ends of a fiber-optic cable costs about 20 dollars per splice.

Let's continue with our discussion of the various broadband technologies before we mention how you and your company can utilize it.

WIRELESS RADIO ACCESS (LMDS)

Of all the broadband technologies that are competing with one another, wireless is my favorite. The technology is simple: Hook a cell-phone-type device to your computer, place a call to your Internet service provider (ISP), and you are connected to the Internet from anywhere. Besides the ability to roam and still be connected, you also won't have to deal with ugly wires everywhere.

This technology is a unique competitor in the broadband space because even though it's not fast enough to be considered broadband, people still want it because wireless access is so appealing. You can surf the Web while watching a baseball game. You can settle a bet with a friend at dinner just by pulling out your cell phone or PDA (personal digital assistant) and checking the

Internet. The potential to save time is what is attracting people to this technology, along with the ability to work, play, and communicate from just about anywhere. If you plan on having an e-commerce site in the future, start looking into wireless technology today. You will need to find out what companies are offering what technology to the consumer. Companies such as AT&T and Sprint have already started talking about holding the Internet in the palm of your hand, and consumers are starting to take notice. Get a few web-ready cell phones and do some investigation for yourself. You will find the phone offers a very limited web interface and requires a different programming language than a normal website.

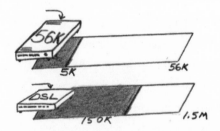

More than likely this will not be a mainstream consumer-level connection for some time. Wireless access is distributed via low-earth orbiting satellites (LEOs) or local multipoint distribution services (LMDs), and current costs are putting this technology in the hands of business customers first. In order for true wireless Internet to reach the consumer, some economical barriers need to be overcome. The consumer is unwilling to pay an unreasonable amount of money to access the Internet. At the same time, the consumer demands a high-speed connection. Well, cheap, high-speed access is not currently what wireless technology has to offer. It's too new and the technology is too expensive. (You might get the "just use your existing computer" line from your spouse if you show him or her the current access price of wireless devices.) This doesn't mean you are off the hook, however. You might want to consider the demographics of the wireless consumer and seriously consider targeting them based on your product. If, for example, your company has an online directory of data that is searchable, whether it's phone numbers, movie listings, addresses, or e-mail, the wireless market is just waiting for you to write a version that will work for them.

Wireless technology is going to be rolling to small devices rather than desktop and portable machines first. The natural dissemination of a wireless Internet is going to be first through devices that are already wireless in nature. Cell phones are the first and most obvious, and they are already appearing on the market. You can surf specific websites, retrieve and send e-mail, get stock updates, find a movie, or do just about anything that involves simple text-based retrieval. They currently don't handle the browsing and viewing of normal websites with any quality because you have no mouse or keyboard for navigation and no hard drive for local information storage. This won't slow down the market impact and penetration that these devices are going to have. Soon, all cell phones are going to offer wireless Internet access (right on the phone) as part of the standard service contract.

Third-party developers such as Macromedia have already demonstrated interactive animation running on such wireless devices. Macromedia is the creator of the Shockwave (streaming M5 driver) technology, which allows streaming flash movies on websites. It (or someone for the company) has ported the M5 streaming flash technology to the Palm PDA and Windows CE. This will allow flash animations to play right on the Palm and Win CE devices. Couple this advance with the new wireless Palm VIII, and you have a wireless Internet connection that can handle animation and interactivity.

Eventually, everything will gravitate toward wireless distribution, but it could be years before we take it for granted. Although it was literally 90 years ago that Nicola Tesla patented wireless electrical energy distribution and constructed the Wardenclyffe tower in New York to wirelessly distribute electrical energy all over the Earth, that has yet catch up to us today. A wireless Internet is a bit less controversial, and moreover, people stand to make a lot of money off it.

Wireless Internet and wired Internet users will both grow, just in different directions. As a company, you should be looking at the total package of what you offer to the consumer—for example, a website. Then find a section of it that should be made accessible to the wireless market, develop it, and offer it to the wireless community. If you've developed a website that is an online encyclopedia, the wired users should get the full experience of it, including sounds, animations, searchability, pictures, and so on. But your wireless users should also be able to access the searchability function of your site. Careful consideration on your part to exactly what the wireless user will and won't use is wise because you will need to have a developer program that is a different version of your site for the wireless market, and this, of course, will cost you money.

ELECTRICAL POWER LINES

Electrical power lines? That's right, the lines that run power into your home could be easily modified to carry Internet data as well. This is a really elegant solution because all you would have to do is plug your Internet device, be it a computer, a laptop, or an Internet-enabled coffeemaker, right into a normal power outlet, and that outlet would provide both 120 volts of power and a high-speed broadband Internet connection to the device.

A company named X10 (www.x10.com) has been doing a mini version of this for years now. X10 offers small devices that you plug into your lamp, toaster, or coffeemaker, which are then plugged into a normal wall outlet. A small box with two knobs lets you dial in the code for that specific device. For example, your bedroom lamp might be "a-1" and your coffeemaker "a-2." Next, you get a control box that can turn on, off, or dim all the devices plugged in. You simply push "a," "1," then "on", and the lamp comes on. X-10 also offers a computer interface that allows you to map out your entire home on the screen and associate it to devices that you can control. So, from the click of a mouse, you can turn devices on or off or even water your yard. Couple this home interface to a broadband network that is distributed via power lines, and you get a completely automated home that can be accessed and controlled by you from the Internet anywhere.

The power company could offer a host of services to consumers with this technology that DSL and cable can't touch, such as remote power-meter reading, power load balancing, and auto service cancellations. Remote power-meter reading could lead to very accurate reports and statistics about how you are using electricity and when, what devices you are using the most, and what your peak times of usage are. Then, if you agree, you could sign up for some type of load-balancing service, where during abnormally high peaks throughout a neighborhood, the power to specific devices in your home could be turned off. While you might not like this idea as a consumer, from a power company's point of view, we can see how this could save money overall.

With an electrical wire Internet connection, devices could automatically access the Internet anytime, with or without you knowing about it. (Perhaps you've seen a commercial on TV where a family is sitting at home when the doorbell rings. The mother answers the door and sees a repair guy with two big toolboxes. The woman says, "We didn't call you." "Nope," the repairman answers, "Big Al called me." Then the woman says, "There's nothing wrong with our refrigerator." The repair guy replies, "Not yet.") The ability for the refrigerator to self-diagnose a problem, connect to a service provider, and dispatch a servicer is what "smart" devices are all about. "Convince through intelligence," we like to call it. The next phase of this same device is keeping your food stocked. For example, your refrigerator could order more orange juice for you, and instead of a repair guy showing up, WebVan does.

The electrical Internet distribution method hasn't been realized yet, and whether it ever will be remains to be seen. The cost is currently in the range of $1500 per customer for the necessary hardware, compared to less than $200 for DSL or cable modems. Not to mention that the technology is still in the testing phase, whereas DSL and cable have millions of combined subscribers.

Currently, the biggest problem is transmission noise—that is, an unwanted signal or disturbance. The transmitting electrical energy creates too much noise for the transmission of Internet data to be effective over distances. However, this could become a viable transmission method within the next five years. Recently, a method of transmitting the Internet data has been discovered that is not in with the electrical signal, but rather around the wires in the surrounding electromagnetic field that all power lines naturally generate.

The broadband world is at our doorstep. Internet developers have been dreaming of a time when they could effectively develop a website or web utility that has the potential to be like an interactive CD-ROM. This is what a broadband connection will allow and does allow right now. Applications that normally just sit on your desktop and never access the Internet can and will begin using the Net for all kinds of helpful things. For example, software could check the Net for an update of itself and automatically keep current. You could be working in Photoshop 5.5 at 5 P.M. on Monday, then double-click the same icon Tuesday morning, and Photoshop 6.0 starts up. Up pops a document listing all the new features you just received for free—just for being such a loyal customer.

Software could also use a high-speed connection to interact with the Net and its resources, giving you the impression that the application you were using was "all knowing." Imagine an encyclopedia application that takes up 1 MB on your hard drive but has every volume of text and every photo right there at your fingertips. The application could be developed as a "shell" that retrieves data from a database that lives on the Internet somewhere. This would allow the developer an incredibly easy way of updating the encyclopedia's content, which means the customer can access a current copy every time he or she starts it up. This could be charged to the customer in many different ways, a one-time charge or a single access charge.

SO, WHAT IS BROADBAND AGAIN?

We realize that this chapter contains a lot of information to digest—especially if you are a nontechnical person, so let's recap. Broadband is a high-speed connection that is being rolled out to the consumer in the current form of DSL and cable modem technologies. DSL and cable modems differ from one another in terms of who is providing the technology and how that providing company implements the technology. Remember, there are lots of ways to build a broadband network. Both of these last-mile solutions are competing against each other for market share, and cable modems are currently ahead.

Planning out a strategy for delivering a site to a customer that has a DSL or cable modem should be your focus. For your business to thrive, you will need to come up with creative ways to utilize the consumers' higher-speed and always-on connection. The customers with broadband connections will seek broadband sites.

There are other broadband technologies such as fiber optics, wireless, and electrical power lines; however, these are still expensive and just starting to get off the ground. Still, they should constantly be in your peripheral business vision because these are the technologies after DSL and cable modems that the consumer will start getting.

Finally, always think creatively. Remember, consumers are attracted to sites that stand out from the others by offering something different, perhaps a broadband and a normal version, and they come back to a site for some convenience it affords them.

CHAPTER 3

Broadband

The Interactive Technologies

This is the fun part. We truly believe that companies that work on the Internet are unknowingly redefining the future of the world's economic, entertainment, and telecommunications industries. Remember all that talk years ago about 500 channels of TV? *Forget that.* The Internet is the TV of the future, and a grand unification of information and technology is rapidly converging to make it possible.

WebTV is the first service that comes to mind here. In case you haven't heard of WebTV, this is the company that Microsoft invested millions of dollars into a few years back. WebTV manufactures a small box that you plug your cable and phone line into and then connect to your TV. Accompanying the setup is a wireless mouse and keyboard. The result is a bizarre mixture of windows that flip around, containing the TV shows you want to watch and their respective websites, or any site. Some TV shows even take advantage of this, providing a "come visit our Web site" blurb, and the WebTV unit presents you with a link that you can use to instantly visit that site. When you do, you see both the website and the TV show, allowing you to buy tie-in merchandise. It's very compelling, highly interactive, and the compulsive buy factor is so high that it is easy to find oneself with a most random collection of things. For example, you could be watching a movie, notice how much you are enjoying the soundtrack, visit a site like Amazon.com to purchase it, and return to the movie in time to see the ending. The only issue with WebTV is that it currently isn't broadband-capable; it only offers a 56-kbps modem connection. However, it's still fun, and it's only a matter of time before a broadband version will be available.

How can a dot com benefit from something like this? Well, first think *multimedia*. Find someone who can blend technologies together that can be distributed via the Internet. If you work in the video industry, hooking up with a flash developer will allow your video to have a top layer of high-quality, vector-based artwork/animation that adds an interactive interface to your video. Instead of being able to start and stop video, your customers could jump to different sections or even pick their own endings. Internet innovation is what will push your company further than your competition. That interactive animation layer could contain "hotspots" that are floating over your video, allowing consumers to click and buy what they are watching. The interactive layer contains all the necessary URL locations and/or shopping cart information for the video layer. Now, it's true that this solution of mixing video and interactivity together would require more bandwidth than a normal modem can handle, but that's the point with a broadband connection.

With broadband, customers will no longer have to wait for websites to download. They can expect video, sound, text, graphics, and photos, all married together in some unique fashion. It's up to you or your multimedia engineers to figure out how to make all the components look good and work well together. Because the Internet can contain and transmit multimedia elements, to take full advantage of it, you must stop thinking in linear terms in your delivery. Although TV is linear—it's just a stream of data that can be turned on or off—the Internet is more like a tree. This unique branching can be used to do things such as show the lyrics of an MP3 that is streaming. (From a commercial angle, you could sell the CD to customers while they listen to samples.) People really want more innovative ideas that fully utilize their broadband potential. Video rental sites could start showing trailers to the movies, or even sell the entire movie in QuickTime format for viewing on the computer.

As all these technologies blend together, the computers of today will become the hybrid communication/learning devices of tomorrow. Your customer will have a communication portal (device) and will expect you to supply such conveniences as interactive video, interactive video games, instant access to TV programs, on-line shopping and banking, the ability to work from home or to take courses, and instant access to music. Everything can be cross-blended with everything else. For example, while watching a show, the viewer could enter "interactive mode" and see items that are for sale on the show. The viewer could buy that jacket or lamp by clicking on it and adding it to a shopping cart. A quick press of a button and the customer can find out if the necessary funds exist in his or her account for the purchase. Starting to see the potential? The true winners are going to be companies that not only "get" the concept, but implement it well. In the above example, a partnership between a bank and a commerce site would have to be established. Customers wouldn't care about how the technology was achieved, but you can bet they would tell a friend if a site had the ability to cross-check the balance of their accounts.

What the broadband consumer is going to be looking for is not an interactive TV. We don't believe that interactive and TV go well together. A TV is a very passive pastime; people like to sit back and do nothing but let the TV entertain them. This is not to say that the TV won't have access to the Web. We just see it being accepted by the consumer as a means to access an unlimited amount of video entertainment sources. A computer, on the other hand, is considered more of an interactive device and is used as a tool for creation and information retrieval and manipulation, like helping with homework, estimating taxes, or getting a good bank loan.

Adding broadband into the consumer arsenal empowers consumers to use the Internet more as an everyday tool. And given a little time, the device will become part of the consumers' normal lifestyle and will be something they can't live without. As mentioned, because of this, we believe that broadband access is really going to be all about businesses taking advantage of the consumers' always-on connection. With web servers and similar technology, you can always be accessible, offering consumers Internet-enabled utilities that perform functions to make their lives easier in some way. The computer industry was founded on the premise that computers would make our lives better and give us all more free time. That is what people are looking for: solutions that are only two steps instead of four.

In short, the Internet is a repository for multimedia content that holds the answers to almost all currently known questions in some fashion, and people want to be able to access that repository of knowledge. It's up to businesses to figure out how to deliver that content to the masses.

In fact, we believe that Internet-enabled applications will fast become more popular than the traditional web browser. Don't get us wrong. The web-browsing pastime isn't going away; however, more useful and strategic methods of delivering information, goods, and services to the consumer will start to emerge in the broadband space. Implementing this type of application correctly will require a programmer versed in Lingo, C, Java, or C++. These languages allow the creation of very robust applications that can interact with data stored on Internet servers anywhere in the world, and the user doesn't need a web browser. Web browsers are "the box," so start thinking outside of them. Both the Macintosh and Windows operating systems can take full advantage of the Internet, and your custom written applications can too.

Imagine having an application named "Amazon" that lives on your hard drive just like Netscape or Photoshop. When you start it, not only are you connected to Amazon.com, but you could be presented with a highly interactive experience that isn't held back by the limitation of web browsers. Another example is online banking. Right now, the number one reason people don't bank online is because they are worried about security. Building a banking application that runs just like any other application will make customers feel more secure; they won't feel like they are submitting sensitive information into the World Wide Web, but rather into an application with menus and windows—similar to Excel. Not only would this help instill confidence, but it would also allow more flexibility, with the possibility of offering the consumers features outside the scope of a browser's abilities.

Obviously, the possibilities aren't just limited to the banking industry. Any and all companies that perform business-to-business (think Cisco), business-to-consumer (think Amazon), and consumer-to-consumer (think eBay) transactions could potentially take this scenario to heart. If you don't evolve and adapt, your company's website creation abilities might no longer be what your client is looking for, and your industry could have turned in a direction for which you weren't ready.

WHAT INDUSTRIES ARE IMPACTED?

If a company ends in "dot com," it will be affected by the broadband revolution. In addition, even companies that are associated with dot coms will feel the effects. If you sell CDs online, for example, your jewel case provider will feel the impact in terms of more orders from you.

Our primary concern here is what industries the new broadband B-to-C (business-to-consumer) market will impact and how. Remember that broadband is about the consumer. The B-to-B market is already working at broadband speed, but the consumer isn't yet. The B-to-C market is where money comes from. Even if your business model is to serve other companies by creating websites for them, you still need to think in terms of the B-to-C relationship. True, your money is coming from another company, but you can bet the company you are working for is concerned about the B-to-C market because that's where their money comes from. And ultimately, if you cannot create a site that brings in the money for your client, it will fire you. Those industries that are playing in the B-to-C market should start looking at broadband technologies and using them to expand their offerings to the consumer right now. When you go to work tomorrow, approach the most technically savvy person you know and ask, "Can we talk about putting together a broadband team?"

BROADBAND CONTENT EVALUATION

Should any of your or your client's content be made into a broadband version? To answer this, consider the following questions:

1. Was the original content (before it went to the Web) scaled, compressed, or down-sampled to make it fit within bandwidth requirements of a modem?
2. Does the site currently use video, audio, or interactivity?
3. Would the site "sell" better with video, audio, or interactivity?

Answering yes to any of these makes the site an ideal candidate for a broadband version.

Any company that has a website or offers the creation of a site needs to seriously look at its content development on a regular basis and realize that there is a big transition coming that it needs to make. The general need of an internal research and development department becomes very evident here. Someone in your company should be tasked with thinking about the future direction of the Internet and all its surrounding technologies, then making monthly direction corrections to your company's efforts. If you are in the business of creating sites for other companies, you might be able to get your client to fund a broadband version of their site. Chances are, if your client is creating a website, they know about broadband already, which will make it easier for you to sell the idea to them. Your goal would be to have a small internal team build a high-bandwidth version of the client's site, or just portions of it, to show off both the potential of broadband and the potential of your company..

The needs and wants of the consumer vary like the ebb and flow of the stock market. Keep in mind, however, that consumers don't really know what they want in terms of technology, and most could care less about it. They do know what they want in terms of merchandise, services, or information. That is what the consumer is really after.

It's often hard to remember this when you are in the middle of a three-month development cycle of a C application that has 100,000 lines of code and interfaces with 10 back-end servers being programmed by 5 engineers. This is where R&D checkups are helpful. During the development cycle of anything for the Web, the team should check in with R&D to make sure the technology is not inhibiting the vision. Think of it this way: R&D is the navigator of your ship. You may be the captain who knows where you are going and technically how to get there, but once you are underway, you could easily lose site of both your departure and destination horizons and end up 20 miles off course. R&D will keep you on course and may offer you information about course corrections and danger signs you weren't expecting. If you work in an environment where R&D isn't possible, then the development of a broadband team should be established. This team should try to develop a site that is broadband-enabled, then disseminate the knowledge of building that broadband site to the rest of the departments.

CONSIDERATIONS

The development of a site for the broadband consumer should include the following:

1. *High-bandwidth content.* A broadband connection can handle about 125 kb of data per second.
2. *Interactivity.* Technologies should include JavaScript, Shockwave, Flash, and Interactive QuickTime.

3. *Larger imagery.* Where appropriate, the images should be bigger.

IMPACT

The first industries that will experience a real economic impact are the telecommunications companies. Obviously, broadband providers are already making money rolling this out in the form of DSL and cable modems. Telecommunications companies are the originators of broadband distribution, so in a metaphoric sense they are droplets of water in the smooth-as-glass pond.

As the ripple expands outward, so too does the broadband innovation. After the telecom companies get their version of a broadband service out to a critical mass number of people, the ripple will move to the consumer. Now, imagine that all the average home consumers have a broadband connection at home. How does the ripple pass on and to whom? Well, the consumer will start gravitating toward sites that offer a more broadband-tailored experience either through advertising or word of mouth. If presented with a choice, consumers will stop using sites that are static and start going to sites that are more dynamic, more interactive, and more fun to use. Why read about a store when you could watch a little news clip about it or listen to an audio clip that describes what it offers? This natural consumer gravitation toward higher-bandwidth sites will inadvertently pass the broadband ripple to companies that develop websites.

Welcome to the future. You are now standing at the edge of that pond, ready for the ripple to come hit the point on shore where you are standing.

The order of industries affected again will be from the communication/telecommunication companies to the consumer to the developers. The telecom companies are already rolling out to the consumer, so it's only a matter of time before the consumer starts looking for higher-speed sites and solutions. Prepare now. Remember the saying "test early, test often." This means being ready for what is to come so you can head off any problems long before they are critical.

Now let's walk through a little scenario.

WEB TEAM SCENARIO

Generally, companies that develop websites have or should have an infrastructure of skilled and talented people in place that includes an account manager to handle the client; a producer to coordinate the internal team members, develop the time line, and handle the workflow; a designer to create the look of the site; a user experience person to create the navigation and the feel for the site; a multimedia engineer to create any interactivity and special effects; and a web engineer to handle the page and server programming. This type of team is necessary to create a high-quality site worth charging hundreds of thousands of dollars. And in most cases, this is just the general type of people you should have, not the quantity. You could easily have four designers, two multimedia engineers, three programmers, and so on, depending on the size of the project or its delivery time line.

Okay, let's imagine you have this type of structure or something close to it. How do you get all these people working toward a broadband direction? If your company is set up like most, someone is always watching the bottom line, such as a general manager or managing partner. These people must be sold on the impending broadband revolution. . Get them a copy of this book and tell them to sleep with it under their pillows because the knowledge will transfer to them via osmosis just like in college. Seriously, companies should envision broadband as a client and fund a few month-long imaginary projects where a site is developed with the intention of delivering a highly interactive and media-rich experience. The experience should be targeted and developed at the bandwidth minimum for a standard broadband user, which is in the neighborhood of 125 to 150 kb of throughput per second (a far cry from the 4.7 kb throughput days of the 56-kbps modem). Remember how compelling interactive CD-ROMs were, with such games as Myst and Iron Helix? Well, they were all targeted at 90 kb or less of bandwidth, so the experience you should be creating should be no less compelling.

 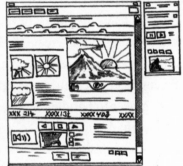

The goal here is to identify problems and strengths and weakness in your organization to learn if you are potentially ready to handle a broadband client or initiative.

Following are the steps involved in building a broadband website:

1. Identify a small group of people from each department.
2. Tell the group bandwidth isn't an issue with this project.
3. Pick a project to develop, or convert an existing site into a broadband one.
4. Identify who is responsible for what on your team.
5. Set development timelines and deliverable dates.

6. Remind everyone again that bandwidth isn't an issue with this project.

7. Create and approve static comps.

8. Design, develop, and program the site.

INTEGRATION INTO COMMON ELECTRONIC DEVICES

Picture this: You are driving to work and you can't remember if you turned off the coffeepot. On top of this, you are late for work and stuck in traffic.

No problem. You pull out your cell phone or PDA, connect to the Net, dial into your home interface control box, and request a power status report. Your interface box can either talk back or transmit a detailed status list, but since you're driving, you have it speak to you. You find out the coffeemaker, the refrigerator, two lamps, the backyard light, and your VCR are all on. With one voice command, "All off," everything is shut off. Your refrigerator is "smart," and knows better than to turn off permanently, reverting to its thermostat controls. You can now make it safely to work without worrying about burning the house down.

Then, when you get to work, you use your computer to log into your home interface control box. By entering your PIN, you are granted full access to all the devices in your home. You know that you're going to be late, so you program your lights to "random" mode, simulating someone being home. And you program your VCR to tape a show you don't want to miss. While you are logged on, your home interface informs you that the light on the third floor near the back closet is burned out and asks your permission to place an order for a new one. This an example of a broadband-enabled home with "smart" electronic devices.

Although other Web-enabled devices may be available at this time, the first one that we've actually seen was a Whirlpool refrigerator that had a small LCD screen on the front door. The screen was an interface to functions that the refrigerator could perform and a link to websites that could help you with recipes and the reordering of items you need. In addition, the link could communicate to the manufacturer any problems with the unit.

Let's look at some devices on the verge of integration, the pros and cons of such devices, and how you can take advantage of them. The first and most obvious is the refrigerator, just mentioned. The web enabling of this device has the potential to make it a similar experience to walking into a store and buying anything you want. If the consumer wants pizza delivered, he or she could go to the refrigerator and place an order. If the consumer is running low on soy milk, he or she could order it and request a delivery time.

On the other end of this scenario is where your opportunity lies. Devices will not only talk to the Net but allow the Net to talk to them. This means that if you are a website developer, you might be given the programming ability to communicate with that person's refrigerator and find out if the person needs to reorder anything. Or, better yet, you can offer the consumer an item to complement something he or she already has—for example, mustard for hot dogs. Other advantages of smart devices include power consumption monitoring and reporting. You could tell your fridge you're going on vacation and program it to conserve energy.

In fact, you could even communicate with it via the Web after you've gotten to your destination.

The phone is next. The standard telephone might not seem like a candidate for a smart device but why not? After all, it's already on the Net, using essentially the same wires. So, what could it do? Well, for starters, it can become the interface to other devices and services. In fact, a programming language already exists called VOXML (voice-activated markup language) that allows a website to be read and navigated by a phone. Not only would this allow the consumers to control their smart devices via their phones, it could also give them access to sending and receiving e-mail, faxes, and all sorts of database functions.

All of these possibilities offer plenty of new business potential. Just using the standard DTMF (Dual Tone Multiple Frequency) tones the phone can produce normally allows control of all types of devices and services. You can already listen to movie listings, check your bank balance, or order tickets to a concert. Once devices and appliances become smart, you will be able to offer services to your customers such as programming the VCR, turning lights off and on, and even watering the lawn. Soon, your customers will be able to control anything that connects to the Web, and your business can take advantage of that by either building devices that are web-ready or smart or by building sites that can talk to those smart devices.

Still another device is the VCR. We still cannot understand why manufacturers haven't already made a VCR that can interface with your phone line so you can program it while you are away. (There must be some universal law that says you will remember a show you wanted to tape only after you leave.) This device has a lot of potential. A VCR could have an internal broadband modem that allows it access to the Net or to your home interface to the Net. Because such a VCR would be able to accept and transmit infor-mation, you could program it, and it would send you data. It could also retrieve information about TV shows. With this setup, you would be able to access the VCR's programming menu via a special web page that allows you to see if a tape is in and how much time remains on it. A programming interface allows you to either choose from a list of shows you programmed into it that you watch regularly or enter some type of VCRPlus code or manually enter the data about a program you want to tape. The VCR could even send you reminders that a program that you normally watch is coming up and request whether to tape it for you.

Currently, the ReplayTV and TiVo devices are the next-generation VCRs. However, they have one drawback. Because there is no removable media, you can't pop a tape or disk out of what you've taped and loan it to a friend who might enjoy it.. While this isn't what they were designed for, perhaps in the future these companies will figure out some solution to this. Both these companies do the same thing except that TiVo charges a monthly subscription fee. These technologies are a combination of innovations on existing technology. For those of you unfamiliar with how these devices work, here is a quick overview. You attach a box to your TV; then you plug it in to the wall outlet and the phone outlet. It calls into a database automatically every once in awhile and downloads a list of available TV programs onto its internal hard drive. Then it presents a menu that allows you to pick the shows you routinely watch. The device records them all using MPEG encoding onto the internal hard drive. Then when you come home from work or a business trip, everything you want to watch is there at the touch of a button. Unlike an analog VCR tape, the shows don't need to be rewound or fast-forwarded through commercials because the hard drive can be accessed nonlineally. One additional feature of these devices is the ability to pause normal TV shows. When you hit the Pause button on a live TV broadcast, the live show is cached onto the hard drive. Then when you hit Play, the hard-drive playback begins picking up right where you left off.

Although these devices aren't broadband devices, they are very close, and they have the potential to make a serious dent in the VCR consumer market share. However, the lack of removable media, which would enable you to transport your taped material to work or give it to a friend, is what is scaring the average consumer away from choosing this device over a VCR. An inside source at ReplayTV informed us that in the future its device could have a sort of a broadband television-on-demand capability added to it. This capability would allow you to search for TV programs and then download them to your ReplayTV unit.

Businesses in the future that are planning on developing or have already developed some type of consumer electronic device should consider what such a device could do for their consumers and business if it were Web-enabled. We think you will find that a Web-enabled version is not only a good direction but the only direction. Businesses that don't see this potential and apply it to their hardware could be put out of business by their competitors that do.

In the world of broadband, Web-enabled devices would thrive with a few adaptations. First, RJ-45 or Ethernet connections must be added, allowing these devices the ability to stream their recorded content to the user. The device could even become a personal entertainment collection and distribution device. Whether you are at home, on the road, or at work, you could access its content via the Web somehow, even in a 320 x 240 format. You should also be able to connect to the device and control it the same way you do the broadband VCR described previously.

Even home appliances that use electricity but don't necessarily need a computer interface, for example, a toaster, still have the potential for business development to make life a little simpler. Simple on-and-off devices such as lamps, irons, toasters, and hot tubs could all be controlled and regulated from anywhere in the world. The connection to and from those devices will need an interface, a website, and some technology solutions to make them function.

BROADBAND ACCESS NETWORK TECHNOLOGIES: ATM

The broadband Internet that is being pushed out to the consumer really could not have been possible without the innovation of ATM (Asynchronous Transfer Mode) technology. This is the communication backbone for all different kinds of broadband devices, from DSL to cable modems. ATM networking was picked to be the broadband delivery standard for many reasons—for one, its integration ability. Currently three types of services come into the standard home: the cable line, telephone lines, and the Internet. ATM technology can handle the merging of all three of these services into one wire.

A visual metaphor for how an ATM network works is a freeway. All the cars are "cells" that travel to and from place to place, never running into each other (hopefully). Each knows where it came from and where it is going. When each cell gets to its destination, it can hand off a piece of information. In a sense, this is how data travels within a broadband network to and from server to client.

The ATM infrastructure is already in place, and telecommunications companies are working to make ATM Broadband networks available to everyone in the form of cable or DSL.

DIGITAL SUBSCRIBER LINE: ADSL

An asymmetric digital subscriber line (or simply DSL) is by far the most robust form of broadband delivery to date because the wire is already in your house, whether you're aware of it or not. You see, DSL technology does to your phone line what a CD did to your cassette tapes. If you have a normal phone line, with no DSL service, you have an analog phone line. The phone company realized that if they converted the analog signal into a digital signal, there would be a lot of free bandwidth left over. And what could be put through that extra bandwidth? You guessed it—an Internet connection. The nontechnical reader at this point might be thinking, how does one phone line carry a voice conversation and an Internet connection simultaneously? In case you didn't know, DSL allows you to be connected to the Internet and talk on the phone at the same time.

In order to spare you some serious technical information about bandwidth splitters, we'll give you an analogy. Picture a tube with water flowing through it. If you add some oil, the two liquids will travel together but never really get mixed up. Thus, at the other end you can easily extract the two liquids again. The DSL wire is similar. Your voice (or water) travels in a specific "area" of the tube and the Internet data (or oil) travels in another section. The DSL wire reaches a "splitter," and the voice and data are separated out, much like one speaker lets you hear both the singer's voice and the drums being played. (Now, a more technically inclined person might think, "How simplistic!" We do have a full understanding of the transmission spectrum of dmt-based ADSL systems. But it's tough to explain concepts like QAM-modulated sub-channel tones that are individually optimized to serve as a function of impairments to someone who might not even have a grasp of the most basic concepts of how a light switch works.)

Your voice (or normal phone conversation) is transmitted from 0 to 4 kHz, and the DSL upstream data consists of modulated subchannels (or sending channels) which fall in the 20- to 140-kHz range while the downstream (or receiving data channels) modulated subchannels fall between 200 and 1000 MHz.

There are three current advantages to DSL: (1) It's here today, (2) it's inexpensive, and (3) if you have a decent phone company, it might actually be able to make DSL work in your home. (We've heard of one case where it took five and six visits from many DSL "engineers" to the person's home to get the technology working. Two modems, a month of doing nothing but waiting, and about five technicians later, the customer had DSL. Granted, his normal phone stopped working for a day or two, but once all the bugs were worked out, he was left wondering how he ever got by with a modem.) The only current downside to DSL is that a digital signal travels through copper wires less efficiently than an analog signal and must therefore originate a very specific distance or less from your home. The current distance is somewhere in the neighborhood of 1.5 miles. This means if your local phone company is farther away than 1.5 miles, you're out of range of the DSL signal. Sorry, Charlie.

VDSL

Digital subscriber lines come in many different flavors, but the technology involved is the same. The difference between ADSL and very high speed DSL is the connection speed involved. ADSL is designed mostly for the home user where downloading data to the computer is more important than sending data. With VDSL, sending and receiving are equally important. The connection speed of an ADSL line usually tops out between 384 kB and 1.5 MB per second, while VDSL can handle up to about 50 MB per second.

Although much slower, at the present time, ADSL is what the typical consumer is buying. However, in two or threes years, VDSL could start picking up in popularity. This would allow you even more bandwidth flexibility in the development of your broadband applications and systems.

CABLE MODEMS

Cable modems are the only broadband technology that doesn't use some arcane acronym. (How could the engineers have missed calling this something like CabMods or CMDs? Don't they realize people might actually be able to figure out what they are saying?) Actually, calling them *cable modems* might have contributed to their successfully installed base numbers. The average consumer would be more likely to get an Internet connection via something that doesn't intimidate them. An *asymmetric digital subscriber line* sounds too much like NASA might have to show up to get this to work.

In addition, the concept of a cable modem is accessible to most people. Hey, you already have cable, right? Let's just hook your cable box your computer. Sounds easy, doesn't it? It is, actually, but there is one little drawback that is still very much of an issue. Picture a neighborhood of houses that all have cable modems and share the single split cable line coming from the telephone pole at the end of the block. Now, in one house Rachel turns on her computer, enables file sharing, and leaves for work, with the intention of connecting to her home machine from work. Enter neighbor two, Oliver, who turns on his computer and by chance looks at either the Network Neighborhood on a PC or the Chooser on the Mac and is surprised to see a shared server named "Rachel's iMac." Oliver selects it and is able to access her computer's files. This could be a major security issue because, while it's true Rachel can password-protect her computer, her printer is unprotected if connected to the same "shared" computer. Oliver can print, reprogram, or even password-protect her printer.

In addition, download speed fluctuates based on the number of neighbors currently using the connection. The concept is similar to the way most big companies are set up. It can be efficient and fast most of the time, but can really be slow at other times. (And, of course, those times always occur when you're in a hurry.)

From the point of view of market share and which device you should target when you are developing a broadband site, you shouldn't worry. Both ADSL and cable modems offer throughputs over 100 kbps, but as consumers learn more about the two technologies, they may start gravitating toward DSL.

FIBER OPTICS

The potential for fiber in the future is gigantic. Fiber optics is just now starting to become recognized as the ultimate method for data communication. In the future, all wires will be replaced by fiber.

Fiber optics is nothing more than a fiber similar to glass, but flexible and with optical characteristics that allow light to travel through it. Because of its flexible nature, it is perfect for snaking through buildings and conduit. Generally, fiber is much, much smaller than a wire, which is normally used to carry data. In fact, a fiber-optic cable the width of a human hair can handle about 50,000 phone calls worth of traffic, whereas a copper wire the width of a human hair can handle one. In the future, fiber-optic manufacturers and providers will be the companies in which to invest.

As you can see, fiber is not specifically a broadband delivery method. However, broadband services such as DSL, cable modems, and large office buildings could not function without having fiber connections.

WIRELESS RADIO ACCESS

The wireless Internet world is almost here. Wireless technology is big in Japan and Europe, and at the moment, the United

States is playing a little catch-up. Wireless Internet data transmission is going to significantly change the way we as humans live and interact with one another. Some might be a bit wary of a world of instant access, inhabited by always-on, always-connected people, but the plus side is strong enough to make us all interested in seeing the outcome of such a world. It's going to happen anyway, so you might as well embrace it.

The current methods of data transmission are similar to the way your cell phone works, except data is transmitted in addition to your voice and the device has a small screen to raster the image. Generally, the device will be a cell phone or some type of wireless PDA, such as the Palm VIII. The type of consumer will be the businessperson on the go who wants to take advantage of wireless services and goods that complement his or her lifestyle. Later, as the cell phone and PDA market come down in price, these devices will be distributed more into the general public. At this point, the web consumer of today will be the wireless web consumer of tomorrow. Not only will offering your website or web services on wireless devices and PDAs be a good idea, but a time will come when all Internet business will move toward the wireless method, as well as the normal "wired" method we now use. Businesses that have only conventional websites and not sites that wireless customers can access will be treated like businesses today that have no websites at all.

ELECTRICAL POWER LINES

The most radical and far-reaching broadband technology is the distribution of Internet data via the national power grid. Of all the broadband technologies that are coming, electrical power distribution has the greatest potential energy. Remember from high school physics that potential energy is nothing until it's converted into kinetic energy. However, this has a long way to go before it can start being kinetic.

The possibilities, including e-commerce, for an Internet world based on its data being sent in combination with the power for the same device are great. However, a lot would have to change before this becomes a viable method of communicating. Computers would have to be modified internally to accommodate a power supply that could split the power and the data and route them to the correct parts of the computer. Or, an external device would have to be created that allowed the computer to plug into it, and that device would then need to be plugged into a special outlet. The power company has an alternative that currently works, but the cost to the consumer is in the neighborhood of $1600 per person, which is outside the range of what most people are willing to pay for a broadband connection.

CHAPTER 4

The Last Mile Deployment Challenges

Y ou want challenges, let's talk about actually building a broadband network. The process of trying to deploy something that no one has ever done before poses a variety of roadblocks, red tape, and configuration issues. For example, let's say you invented the concept of digitizing the analog signal that phone conversations travel on and could see in your mind's eye the potential that innovation had. First, you would need to fully understand what it is you had your hands on and its potential. You would need to sell your idea internally to your research team and ultimately to the person that makes financial decisions within your company. As you spec out the mathematical potential on paper, the concept becomes more and more exciting. You can actually see this idea coming to life, and you can start to glimpse a future where connecting to the Internet could be hundreds of times faster.

Now say that you have this idea that works on paper, and you casually refer to it as a "broad bandwidth" connection in trying to explain it. You propose the plan like this: "Would you fund an initiative where we could handle a hundred times more data through a standard copper phone wire?" The financial manager is definitely interested. But now that you've been given the okay, you need to build this thing.

STARTING FROM SCRATCH

Obviously, broadband isn't a tangible item you can hold in your hand, but your goal is to create something that is real and accomplishes the high-speed connection of your dreams. The first phase involves concepts on paper that prove mathematically correct. This thing has to work inside and out, forward and backward, and side to side before you actually start picking up a screwdriver.

The idea here is to digitize the analog signal and see what type of bandwidth is really in a copper wire. The traditional method of delivering a telephone conversation over the Internet is by way of electrical pulses that travel through copper wires. A sound current is passed through a wire that also passes through a microphone and a speaker. As the microphone is spoken into, air from your voice pushes on a small element in the microphone that disturbs the flow of electricity, thus affecting the flow in the entire wire. At the other end, the speaker reproduces the sounds of the disturbance by reversing the process. The speaker pulsates in and out at the same frequency at which the microphone was spoken into. Then the speaker pushes on the surrounding air to produce sound. This is how sound travels through a copper wire.

But how do two computers speak to one another? Glad you asked, because the next step that brings us closer to the advent of broadband is the ability for computers, which are digital, to communicate with one another via an analog phone infrastructure that is older than computers. Enter the modulator/demodulator, or modem for short. The modem was a technological breakthrough around 20 years ago. Anyone who was ever really into computers for business of any kind ran out and purchased the superfast 300-baud modem. (At the time they were still called the "acoustic coupler device." Great marketing. Only the most technically savvy would buy them because they were attracted to technologically complex devices.)

At this time, connecting to computer bulletin board services (or BBSs) was all the rage. Users found additional uses for their Commodore Vic-20s other than writing BASIC programs that moved the asterisk from one side of the screen to the other. The BBSs allowed users to connect to another computer using the home phone line and post messages for other users to read—a true electronic bulletin board. (Could the inventors of this possibly have envisioned a broadband type of connection in the future?) But how did that little acoustic coupler work its magic?

Many of us have known for a long time that computers were digital, and phone lines were analog. If you've ever taken apart a 300-baud modem, you would have found simply a speaker, a microphone, a loop of wire, a little power transformer, and a small circuit board. This device was in essence taking a range of numbers and making them audible tones. The tones would vary their pitch to correspond with a different number. If, for example, the computer wanted to send a "1," the modem made a specific and unique sound. The modem had the ability to do two things: "listen" (or receive) or "speak" (or transmit). When two computers needed to establish a connection with one another, a series of "hello" tones were sent that would put the other computer into a listening state.

Then the two computers would pass back and forth a series of tones that set up connection protocols such as the speed at which to communicate. The data that you wanted to send was collected and batch-transmitted in a long continuous series of tones.

TURNING UP THE THROTTLE

A speed of 300 baud was considered "neat." The next-speed modem, 1200 baud, had people saying "really neat." But, it wasn't until the 9600-baud modem that people start saying "wow." About this time, businesspeople began to get enthusiastic. People started understanding that connecting computers to one another was a way to communicate and pass more than just typed text, like the BBS days offered. People could now pass pictures, files, applications, and sounds. Around this same time, America Online started to become popular, in part because of the speed that the 9600-baud modem offered and the fact that it was the one of the few places to connect to when you used your modem.

The 9600-baud rate was the norm for a long time, and people just understood that this was the speed at which computers communicated via modem. But just as fast as computers doubled their processor speed, another modem came out that was touted as twice as fast as the 9600-baud modem. The 14.4-kbps modem sent everyone to the computer store once again. The 28.8 followed, again promising a connection twice as fast as its predecessor. Eventually people realized that modems would continually get faster until data was transferring in real time everywhere throughout the world. The 33.6-kbps modem came out, followed by the 56-kbps. K-Flex and X2 modems soon entered the market, and the consumer was hit with a bit of rather shocking news: The 56-kbps modem is as fast as modems would ever get. (In fact, we can remember friends worrying about the long-term viability of their jobs in part because of the 56-kbps limit. They would have been even more upset had they known that the modem actually had a "potential" effective throughput of 56 kbps, but the 24-gauge copper wires that all homes have can actually support only 53 kbps.)

So, that was it. For years nothing more was said about modems and they continued to be used throughout the computer industry. Everyone had them, and they worked. But was this really it? After all, it still took a long time to download a picture or sounds, and video was next to impossible to download. Someone had to be able to figure out something, right?

Someone did. Around 1995 we started seeing devices in forward-looking magazines like Popular Science that promised to revolutionize the future of home computing by offering almost unlimited bandwidth. Later, the device became know as the cable modem, and rumors started flying about how amazing it was. A buzz ensued about high-speed connection and the ramifications of such an environment, including whether people at home would even utilize a tenth of that kind of speed. Meanwhile, the public was screaming for bandwidth. Companies were trying to figure out if this was a viable venture to undertake, whether it was cost-effective, and whether the device actually worked. The answer was yes on all counts.

HOW DO MODEMS AND DSL WORK?

Earlier in this chapter, we used the scenario of building a broadband network from scratch. People want it; companies see the potential. Okay, so how did companies build it?

The first step was figuring out how to find hidden bandwidth on copper wires that max out at 53-kbps modem voltage levels. Modems work by sending audible signals to and from each other, then converting that sound into a digital signal. Since both computers are digital, the best solution would be to set up a wire connecting the two that passed the data digitally rather than via the current analog format. This was fairly easy to do and is analogous to the digitizing of an analog audiotape into the CD format. Using a technique called *sampling*, the computer records the electrical analog impulses on a cassette tape. The computer samples the voltage levels of the analog signal 44,100 times per second and assigns a value between –255 and 255 to that sample. When played back, the computer simply spits out that same voltage snapshot, and the speaker moves the same way it did with the analog tape. The reason for a negative number is that a speaker moves the air by pushing on it or pulling on it, but its initial resting state is zero.

There is just one last step to complete the process. The digital signal that computers pass to and from each other must travel via the existing phone line that *also* carries the normal analog phone conversations. The solution proved to be that the entire connection from your computer to the phone company's central office had to be digital. This would allow the bandwidth the copper wire provided to be shared with two digital signals: the computer's data and your voice and the voice of the person you're talking with. This was the perfect solution and actually allowed the two connections (the phone and computer) to be handled separately, giving you the added ability to use both devices at the same time.

Both DSL and cable modem technologies work by digitizing the signal, thereby opening up the bandwidth that the physical wire can handle. Let's compare the speed of DSL to a cable modem in terms of baud. A 28.8 modem can send 28,800 bits of data per second, a 33.6 modem can send 33,600 bits of data per second, and so on. We also have the ISDN line, which was the first incarnation of the digital line (actually called the *integrated digital subscriber line*), which can handle data at 128,000 bits, making it in essence a 128-kbps modem. Then you have DSL and cable modems that can handle 1,500,000 bits per second, making these 1.5-Mbps modems, or in terms of kb, 1500 kbps.

The speed is just astronomical, and the experience is smooth and feels more like the rate your body is naturally accustomed to, rather than being constantly left in a wait state every now and then, staring at your screen.

THE RACE

Now that the technology was created, field-tested, and ready for deployment to the consumer, something interesting happened. All of a sudden, the cable company had visions of the phone company delivering video to the consumer, and the phone company had visions of the cable company delivering phone service to the customer. After all, they both now had more than enough extra bandwidth to play with. The race was on.

In a nutshell, the race concerns the rapid deployment of the broadband technologies to the consumer, and the winner will be the one the consumer ultimately uses most frequently. Cable companies have a fairly commanding lead with the cable modem, but this doesn't make them better. First is usually never best. For example, remember the 3DO player, created by the 3DO Corporation? It was a game console that you hooked to your TV, put in a CD, and played video games on. The idea was compelling and the device itself had an interesting design, but it was expensive and slow. Needless to say, 3DO no longer exists, yet the Sony PlayStation is the exact same thing—only refined, well-marketed, and offered at a much lower price.

Although we don't think the cable modems will go out the same way 3DO did, it's important to point out that there is always room to do something better. DSL is a strong example of this. Because cable and phone companies both have the same technology, it's now up to the consumer to decide. AT&T is running ads suggesting that consumers switch to digital cable because they will receive more channels and Internet access. Local phone companies are fighting back with ads of their own suggesting that consumers not get digital cable modems because everyone on their block can share the connection speed. Who will win? Who should you bet on?

Although many of you may be reading this book from a stock market perspective, we recommend that you don't even try taking a gamble on one or the other. A safe bet is keeping an eye on all the players, but no one specifically is going to win here. The real winner will be the consumer, because of the competition created in this space, which ultimately leads to lower prices and technological improvements. And, of course, it's going to be the consumer market share that determines the winner and loser. We do believe that both DSL and cable modem technology will be around together for along time. Both are very good at what they do and both deliver what the customer expects, if not more.

The true race between the two industries will happen in terms of advertising. Whoever markets their products or services better, stronger, and faster than the other will start to gain market share. Currently, the local provider Pacific Bell is targeting AT&T's cable modems with its DSL service, suggesting that, in essence, as more people in your neighborhood connect, your connection slows down. The spot humorously shows neighbors at war with each other for bandwidth, with scenes of cutting flowers, cable lines, and so on. The police have to intervene to hold back the angry neighbors from one another. The entire spot is shot in the style of the television show *COPS*. This very funny spot speaks right to the weakness of the cable modem market. Sure modems are great, and you'll get one. Then someone else on your block will get one, and then another and another. Then you'll find yourself stuck with a connection that is slow.

This is great marketing, and the ads do speak the truth about the technology. However, in actual field tests of cable modems, most neighborhoods that were loaded with cable modems reported that yes, in fact, the speed did fluctuate, but those that responded said that the speed varied from "superfast" to "fast." The thing to keep in mind is that the quality of the service provided really sets the tone for your connection. Small local phone companies might not be able to service you as well as the larger ones, but then again, you might get more attention to detail from them. Another group that was asked about cable modems said they didn't experience any speed fluctuations at all and knew that their neighbors had the same service. They did report that the service was either "superfast" or "not working."

A HORROR STORY
WITH A HAPPY ENDING

DSL has its share of problems, too, but none that are not simply inherent in rolling out a new technology. The initial problem was getting the staff up to speed on actually understanding how to install DSL into a consumer's home. One story we've heard is a perfect example of the difficulty that can sometimes be encountered. This person's local phone company sent an installer out after he passed the "do you fall within the DSL range" check (they run on your phone number). After passing the test, the customer was informed that the central office was close enough to his home for him to receive DSL. The only trouble was he had to wait for the installer for about two to three weeks. This was frustrating, since friends of his already had the technology; not only was he feeling left behind, but he needed a DSL connection for working at home.

Finally, his day arrived. The installer came with two big boxes and a big toolbox. He proceeded to work for four hours in the customer's garage, bedrooms, and phone closet installing jacks, pulling wire, and swearing every now and then. Afterward, he informed the customer that because the customer's computer was a Mac, he would have to do the CPU configuration himself. Then the installer dropped the bomb: "I mean DSL isn't available in your area." The customer then had about two seconds to question him as he quickly packed his bag and headed for his truck. The installer simply told the customer to call the office in a few months to see if DSL would become available in his area soon.

The customer was left feeling he had wasted four hours, plus all the on-hold and web registration time. Shortly after, his wife noticed the phone had no dial tone, just a lovely hum. Another 30 minutes on hold got the customer to an operator who was very understanding. The next day a real service guy showed up, wearing an open shirt with the gold chains and a serious leather tool belt that the customer said looked like one he had bought on his own because he just loved his job so much. The customer thought to himself, "This is the man." He looked as if he was ready to start a fight with anyone that talked bad about DSL. This guy came in like Mr. Spock in the original Star Trek movie and rewired the warp drive engine. He rewired the setup and told the customer he was all set to make the jump to light speed. So the dial tone was restored, but the customer still didn't have DSL service because the first tech took the DSL modem with him. The customer spent a good five days on the phone with every person he could find trying to explain his situation. Nothing worked; no one could grasp the fact that two installers came out, one saying nothing works for you and the other saying everything is fine. It just left the customer in the perpetual state of nowhere. He gave up.

Two months went by and the person was holding a group meeting with the department of engineers that he supervises. They were all saying their DSL service was something they couldn't live without and wondering how they ever got by without it. That made up his mind; he was determined to get it this time. Once again, the customer went through the sign-up process, and a technician arrived, installed the hardware, and was gone within 30 minutes. After he left, the customer felt like living dangerously, so he connected to the Internet and started downloading a file, while he placed a call to his wife. "Guess what I'm doing?" the person asked her. "I'm downloading a file!" She was very excited for her husband, but he knew this was nothing new to her because she had had DSL months before him at work. His life was complete, or so he thought.

A few days went by before his wife and he noticed a problem. When he was using the DSL line, she couldn't use her computer and connect to AOL using its modem. So he would have to disconnect from the DSL and let her use it. Then they noticed that when his wife was on the modem, he couldn't connect to the Net via DSL. He thought of some technical reason as to why this might be normal and forgot about it, until he asked his wife if she ever tried using both her DSL and PowerBook modem. "Yup, all the time," she said. *For the love of God*, he thought.

Needless to say, two very sly technicians came out and fixed it all. And now the customer is an extremely happy customer. In fact, he says that when connected he often asks himself, *How did I ever get by without this before?*

Fortunately, this case isn't the norm. Most who have DSL had it installed without a hitch. Yet this experience highlights the real-world deployment challenges that "last-mile" companies are faced with. It may look great on paper, it may be blazing fast in the lab, and it may be a big hit in the initial field trials, but when the technology is rolled out to the masses, it is at the mercy of the weakest link—the installer who actually has to make this super-hyped-up technology work right in front of you.

THE PLAYERS

A lot of companies, even some individuals, are trying to enter this broadband space by either starting from scratch by building a company from the ground up that has all the latest technology and all the right people, or if an existing company, by buying other companies and trying to form a broadband superforce. At this point, there is no definitive way to tell which method is going to prove better than the other. However, keep in mind that companies that start from scratch have the added advantage of being able to do it right from the get go, whereas companies that buy other companies have the burden of a merger integration to deal with, in addition to trying to figure out how their two (or more) technologies are going to actually work together.

Many companies have recognized the money-making potential of broadband and have either redeployed their existing workforce or purchased a company with the technology to implement it or to teach existing staff. One big acquirer is a company named SBC Communications, a Texas-based company that has acquired Pacific Telesis and Southern New England Telephone. SBC has a global presence with close to 40 million access lines and 7 million wireless customers. In 1999, SBC announced it was going to deploy the DSL line like no one has ever before. Its intention is to connect almost nine million home users and one million businesses to the DSL service. It also has its hands in the satellite market, working with DirecTV to bring some type of service to its members.

Note: There are a lot of other players that are global, and most of them have millions of subscribers connected via access lines or wireless means. It's not our intention to present the pros or cons of any company here, rather we aim to give you a picture of the bigger players in the field. If you are interested in doing business with any one of these companies, you should, of course, conduct your own market research on them.

Ameritech is a company similar to SBC that also has close to 40 million access lines and 7 million wireless customers. It provides cellular, long distance, paging, video feeds like cable, e-commerce, and more. More specifically going after the cable side of the broadband market, this company currently has more than 100,000 cable subscribers. Bell Atlantic Corporation, a telephone access line provider, has upwards of 50 million telephone access lines and close to 9 million wireless customers worldwide. It has made progress in the broadband arena by attempting to offer video entertainment via DSL, with a subsidiary company called Bell Atlantic Video that is working with DirecTV and US Satellite Broadcasting service.

Bell South is another company that has explored video delivery using a broadband network. Previously, it was working with a fiber-to-home solution but ended up choosing a wireless distribution system over it. We assume the fiber method proved to be too cost-prohibitive. However, the decision is still a bit surprising. After all, Bell South has close to 25 million access lines and 5 million cellular customers to play with in a broadband network.

Not all broadband companies get it right the first time out of the gate. An example of this is US West. This company had a broadband video strategy where it was to enter into a partnership with Time Warner Entertainment. The two companies were planning on building a broadband cable network together. Later, US West announced that it had sued Time Warner for its acquisition of Turner Broadcasting. Today, however, US West is currently offering VDSL video access to their customers. They have close to 17 million access lines and about 20 to 30 thousand DSL customers.

MULTIPLE SYSTEM OPERATORS

When a cable provider offers its services in more than one geographical area, it is considered a multiple system operator, or MSO. The number of MSOs in 1952 was 70, and 10 years later, there were 6600, with a combined total of 32 million subscribers. Currently, there are close to 12,000 companies, with 60 million combined subscribers. Some of the largest companies within the

MSO group are TCI Group, Cablevision, Continental Cable, Cox Communications, and Time Warner.

TCI is a large 30,000+ company that has about 15 million customers. It is entering into an interesting broadband space with ventures with Sega and Time Warner. Together, the three are creating the Sega Channel, where customers will be able to find all types of entertainment. TCI also has a global presence, with programming in Europe, Latin America, and Asia.

Next up is Cablevision, which has almost 3 million television customers in 19 states and owns many cable channels. It has launched a broadband high-speed multimedia service to a large number of homes in the New York area and expects to continue to keep expanding this offering to additional subscribers in the future. Another company, Continental Cable, has over four million subscribers and has played a role in developing TV programming like C-SPAN. It also owns Viewers Choice, the biggest pay-per-view service in the United States. Continental has its hands in the satellite service business partnering with PrimeStar, which could be used as their broadband distribution service to some degree in the future.

Yet another satellite-interested company is Cox Communication. It too is interested in direct-to-home satellite programming and multimedia services and is a big player in the wired access line space, with about 3.5 million customers. It provides cable television, telephone, and personal communication services (PCS).

The nation's second-largest MSO is Time Warner, with nearly 12 million subscribing customers. This company isn't just talking about broadband; they have installed fiber optics into the telephone business arena and they launched the Full Service Network (FSN) a few years back. In Florida, customers of this service have a true video-on-demand service that can be controlled just like a VCR, allowing the customer to pause, back up, and fast-forward video delivery.

All of these companies are currently leading the "back-end" efforts of the broadband revolution. Once they establish equilibrium among each other and the winners and the losers emerge within the space, we will start to see a more global connection of people through a wide range of service offerings from these companies.

GLOBAL UNIFICATION

The stage is set for a global unification of information and data sharing. In the future, when the head-to-head competition starts to cool off and a few players emerge, they will control a large percentage of the flowing of data. Sure, there will be smaller providers here and there that claim to deliver data better, but at a more expensive price. The delivery of data may become a controlled and regulated quantity that investors might be able to buy into in some fashion, either through stock or access line leasing.

Once the delivery of data reaches this proportion, where, for example, about 50 percent or more of homes are broadband-capable, a unification of people can start emerging because of it. Obviously, the ability right now to communicate using a computer is more advanced than it was five years ago, but five years from now the computer will be thousands of megahertz and the connection to the Internet (if we still call it that) will be even faster than the broadband connection of today. Your computer will blend together music, video, device control, personal communication, commerce interactions, and education.

The global unification idea is already evident today and is composed of two parts. The first part is the back-end provider's perception of it, and the second part is the consumer's. The back-end provider that has control over the most access lines and wireless subscribers will be considered the global unifier of information and data flow. The consumer, on the other hand, will experience this unification as a global way to interact with other humans.

The connection to other people is just one part of this equation. The ability to access information that is global is the really exciting part. Imagine using the Web to access and learn about information from another countries' libraries. To currently do this, you would need to be able to speak that country's native language. With the global unification system in place, perhaps you won't have to because information could be translated for you.

Yet these are all possibilities that are only reachable once two major events occur. First, the challenges of rolling out broadband networks must be accomplished, and second, developers worldwide must start developing systems, applications, and tools that use the newly built broadband network.

MEETING THE CHALLENGES

As you can see, implementers of broadband face many challenges, from actually building networks to hiring capable people that can install the hardware. Businesses need to constantly evaluate the progress of broadband technologies and the market share it is gaining on a regular basis. Don't get us wrong, though. Broadband is coming, but it's not here yet. Consumer awareness about broadband is what your business must pay attention to. Watching the market share that cable modems and DSL is gaining is as simple as watching the installed base numbers climb over time. As the installed base gets higher and higher, the consumer demand for broadband content will start to rise.

As the consumer demand for broadband starts picking up more speed, the major players will start jockeying for position. Individual companies can get a jump by developing broadband applications, websites, and smart devices today to prepare for the coming inevitable future.

Palm

Connection without wires

www.palm.com

In the early 1990s, the personal digital assistant market came on the scene, but it wasn't perfect. It was in great need of a good product. Those that were for sale were either a huge clunky mess or weren't sophisticated enough, ending up in the bottom of drawers or relegated to being an address book. Then in the mid 1990s came a lightweight, compact piece of digital glory that essentially fit in the palm of your hand—the Palm Pilot™ connected organizer. Today the Palm™ handheld computer is the de facto standard industry accessory, placed strategically on top of conference tables along with cell phones for all-important meetings. Palm, Inc., which spun out of 3Com and has since gone public to a much successful IPO on the stock market, is currently one of the cutting-edge companies creating hand-held devices that incorporate wireless technology, bringing the Internet to the palm of your hand.

Out of all of the various hand-held devices Palm creates, the Palm VII™ hand-held, which debuted in May 1999, was one of the first mainstream wireless devices that connected a user to the Internet, anywhere. (The others have add-on wireless modems.) Because of its built-in radio technology, with a flip up of the antenna and tap of the screen, a user can be instantly connected to a variety of websites such as Fodor's Restaurant and Hotel Reviews, Bank of America, ESPN, ABC News, Ticketmaster, and more. Also Yahoo! Mail and Yahoo! Messenger will soon be bundled with the Palm III™ and Palm V™ hand-held computers. Plus, with the company's Palm.Net™ service, a small monthly fee allows customers to use the Palm service to access the Internet and e-mail.

"Devices like the Palm VII are changing the way people use and interact with the Internet, " says Ted Ladd, Platform Evangelist, Palm, Inc. "We see the emergence of wireless hand-held devices to be one of the major ways in which the Internet will become seamlessly integrated into people's busy lives." As the popularity of Palm's wireless device increases, the public's perception of the Internet is begining to change. No longer is going on the Internet something reserved for time at the computer; rather, the notion of the "Internet" is taking on a different meaning here—freedom. Wireless technology is allowing users instant access when they need it, wherever they need it. This redefinition of the Internet will help get us all closer to the world of broadband.

Of course, Palm's not just popular with consumers. The company can also boast that it has about 50,000 developers, and this number is growing. Developers for the Palm are producing software applications that run on the Palm Operating System (Palm OS®)with applications that include stock tracking, medical services, delivery distribution, travel software, games, and the list goes on. With the strong force of developers and their clear lead into the wireless Internet market, Palm is a step ahead of the competition, mainly Windows CE. Just think, one day you'll be at the doctor's office, and the doctor will have your whole medical chart on file in a Palm hand-held, sending your prescriptions via e-mail directly to the pharmacy, which of course will be ready for pick up by the time you leave the doctor's office. Devices like Palm hand-helds confirm that technology is getting smaller and smarter at the same time.

Wireless technology is still at its early stage of development. But with innovative products like the Palm hand-held computer, the adoption of "smart" devices in our near future will in turn become staples in our lives, both as working professionals and also as a society, as the line between technology, the Internet, and daily life begins to blur.

PART TWO

The Impact of Broadband

CHAPTER 5

The World and the Economy

W ith the world awaiting the digital future, already the broadband revolution is starting to create some strange bedfellows. The huge merger of Time Warner and AOL has created a major buzz in which people suddenly realize how important content is in addition to the broadband delivery method. Alliances are forming with Microsoft and Maytag, mergers are happening, for example, Excite and @Home, and quirky partnerships are forming, for example, William Shatner and priceline.com.

However, as new definitions and new economies are taking place, these partnerships, mergers, and acquisitions are a part of the mad rush to get ahead of the competition. Non-Internet-related companies want a piece of the online world, and Internet companies want the established business experience of offline companies.

This isn't just happening in the United States. Partnerships are being made between countries, truly making the future of broadband Internet a global industry. Companies are realizing not only that positioning themselves as leaders in this revolution nationally but having a stake at the global broadband future will give them more return on their investment and a greater share of the market.

MERGERS AND ACQUISTIONS

One of the biggest acquisitions so far in this digital economy, the AOL and Time Warner merger, was made chiefly with broadband in mind. More specifically, it's the coupling of content and delivery. The $183 billion deal gives AOL the opportunity to become one of the early distributors of broadband because Time Warner owns about 20 percent of the cable systems in the United States. Time Warner is also one of the biggest owners of content, ranging from print magazines (*Time*, *People*), music (Warner Music), television (CNN, HBO), websites (CNNi, various magazine sites), and movies (Warner Bros. Studios, New Line Cinema). Together with AOL's customer install base as America's number one Internet service provider audience, the two companies now as one will play a major role in the upcoming broadband revolution. Dubbed one of the "New Economy Titans" in the January 24, 2000 issue of *Business Week* magazine, Chairman Steve Case of the newly formed Time Warner/AOL explains the role of the new company in the future of broadband: "We're now at the cusp of a fundamental new Internet experience, enabled by broadband access. . . . It's [about] a whole range of experiences, including a more engaging multimedia experience on a whole range of devices, of which TV is increasingly prominent."

Broadband initiatives are already starting through AOL. One of the distribution methods that started in June 2000 is a special AOL service via the WebTV set-top box. Also, the April 2000 launch of AOL Plus gives those AOL subscribers with high-speed access the ability to view special multimedia content. Stakes with

Time Warner's existing cable service, the high-speed cable ISP Road Runner, deals made previously through AOL with satellite companies (AOL owns a stake in DirecTV)—even talks with phone companies about DSL—will start the foundation for not only Time Warner/AOL's broadband future, but the majority of the nation's as well.

In fact, as all of us in the professional world are trying to figure out what will be the best method for delivery (DSL, wireless, and eventually, fiber optics), Time Warner/AOL is all over the board in every possible delivery method, knowing that at least one of those delivery methods will make it. Should that make us business professionals worried? No, because Time Warner/AOL's vision is the adoption of broadband. Their vast exposure in various media industries secure their place in the broadband future no matter what. Most likely, whatever technology they choose to use, it will be the one through which the widest consumer audience will get their first taste of broadband.

What does this mean for the future of broadband? It means that the masses will soon be able to see it and live it faster than you think. AOL is the top ISP in the country, with a subscriber base at an astonishing 20 million and growing. That's not to say that in the future we'll all be accessing broadband Internet with AOL. Actually, Time Warner/AOL has agreed to open up their cable lines to other ISPs. (How much they will charge other ISPs is another story.) What this merger is doing, and what it will do, is start the rapid action to reach the last mile. Other companies will be motivated to work harder and faster to get the broadband delivery method in place. People are starting to hear about broadband and its potential when in normal situations they wouldn't. Time Warner/AOL is preaching broadband to the masses, and people are listening.

While Steve Case is an advocate for open access on cable lines, will his stance change now that he owns part of the stake in the cable world? Case says no, as he lobbies in Congress. Other ISPs hope that with cable under its belt, AOL won't suddenly change its mind and not allow open access at all or make it extremely difficult for ISPs to use their cable lines. The details of Time Warner/AOL's approach for opening up its own cable lines has yet to be determined, and ISPs are concerned that the fine print will actually deter them from entering such agreements.

Case is following the model made by another mega-merger of content and distribution, Excite@Home. However, in the Excite@Home case, the company gives the cable providers a high-percentage stake in the company and control on the board of directors. Now with AT&T Cable having a 74 percent voting stake in the company, there's sure to be a movement to reorganize the cable mess. The cable debate continues on, with politics and business setting the pace for how broadband is distributed.

WHAT DOES THIS ALL MEAN IN THE GLOBAL DIGITAL ECONOMY?

Across the globe, Time Warner has staked their claim in Spain, investing $35 million in February 2000 in Spain's leading digital broadcaster, Canal SatÈlite Digital. With so many local companies having a share in other international companies, it gets difficult at times to find out where you are now that every company's strategy becomes a global strategy for broadband. If you think it gets confusing in the United States, prepare yourself for more kinds of the same confusion around the globe. Others are doing megadeals as well, all hoping to shape and move the Internet economy in a beneficial position for their company, whether they are involved in satellites, telecom, cable, or television. Most of the world is playing one big chess game, strategically moving their pieces in order to figure out ways in which they can be the first to say "checkmate."

As you can see in the graph, Internet usage around the world is growing at a steady rate. Leading the list is the United States, Canada, and Sweden, with the highest percentages of people online based on the overall populations. As deals start happening, don't be surprised if in the next few years an entrance into the Asian market happens, particularly into China because of its superhigh population rate.

Internet Usage in the Top 15 Countries

	Online Population	Total Population	Percentage of Total Population on Line
U.S.	110.8	273	40.6%
Japan	18.2	126	14.4%
U.K.	13.9	59	23.6%
Canada	13.3	31	42.9%
Germany	12.3	82	15.0%
Australia	6.8	19	35.8%
Brazil	6.8	172	4.0%
China	6.3	1,247	0.5%
France	5.7	59	9.7%
South Korea	5.7	47	12.1%
Taiwan	4.8	22	21.8%
Italy	4.7	57	8.4%
Sweden	3.9	9	43.3%
Netherlands	2.9	16	18.1%
Spain	2.9	39	7.4%

Source: The Industry Standard, www.thestandard.com
Computer Industry Almanac, Central Intelligence Agency
Total Population Data are July 1999 Estimates, Figures in Millions

While most of the activity is in the United States, there are groundbreaking deals happening all around the globe that will affect the digital economy here. (Check our website, www.lastmilebook.com, for related global resource links.) Understanding what's happening around the world will give you a better sense of broadband's place in the world, as you narrow your focus straight back to your company. Although technology gets even more confusing overseas with governmental and regulatory issues, you can see that for the most part, this movement will shake itself out and the winners will become the leaders in the broadband revolution. Although a lot is happening all over the world, the two key places to focus on is the activity in Europe and Asia.

EUROPE

The United Kingdom and France currently dominate the European market. Because of the governmental regulation on telephone lines, wireless access has become the major proponent in pushing broadband access. In 1999, 28 percent of the population of Europe already had cell phones. In fact, it's not surprising to find cell phones replacing actual phones in people's homes.

British Sky Broadcasting, or BskyB, the United Kingdom's leading pay-TV service, is all over the map, making deals with other leading U.K. or European companies for online broadband ventures. Deals include online betting/sports channels through Ladbrokes (owned by Hilton Hotels), as well as an agreement with the U.S.-based TiVO to launch the set-top box service in the United Kingdom. British Telecom is also dealing with BSkyB to distribute broadband access via cable lines. Rupert Murdoch, the chairman of News Corp., is also a ubiquitous presence, with investments in global satellites in the United Kingdom and in Asia. His plan? To create "a global platform" for the distribution of digital goods— high-speed content and services that will include e-mail, movies, commerce, and TV. Murdoch is also in talks with Microsoft and Yahoo!, which would give them stakes in News Corp.

Although the market is set to go forward with broadband, uses may not be connecting with a standard PC. According to Forrester Research, more than a quarter of European adults online will connect to the Internet via non-PC devices by 2003. For the most part, you can bet that the wireless revolution that will fuel broadband in Europe will be wireless technology.

ASIA

By 2003, both Japan and China will be the leaders in Asia for online use, with about 43 million people. With Japan's high-tech knack for products and China's huge population, the two countries will have a strong effect over the way in which broadband makes its way to users' homes.

Using software that combines the TV with the telephone, in the summer of 2000 Japanese shoppers will be able to talk and shop directly with salespeople at their favorite stores, all through their TV. U.K. firm Media Logic is providing their iSee technology to 15 Fujitsu cable operators, allowing for the interactive home shopping experience. Because business in Japan is typically conducted face-to-face, this gives consumers the reassurance that their needs are being met.

Not surprisingly, getting online in China is not so easy. Because it's a communist country, the government is regulating the content on news sites to filter out the "harmful" content. But the Hong Kong–based web portal company china.com, which provides web advertising services with 24/7 Media Hong Kong, as well as web consulting, runs four sites: taiwan.com, hongkong.com, cww.com, and china.com. It already has two million subscribers and will give content providers such as Excite@Home a run for their money should they enter into the broadband delivery market.

But don't forget how Rupert Murdoch is becoming a big player in the Asian market. As owner of Hong Kong's STAR TV, Murdoch is strategically placing himself all over the globe. HKT, Hong Kong's cable and wireless giant and its leading telecom company, is partnering up with Murdoch's STAR TV to provide interactive TV and broadband Internet to the city in late 2000. Murdoch's key position in both satellite and cable companies will position him as one of the leading figures in the broadband revolution. STAR TV is also looking at ways in the next year it can provide services to India in the future.

SECURING
BROADBAND COMMUNICATIONS

As the broadband grows around the world, so does the concern for security of personal data on local computers. Issues of security are important because the more data we will transmit in the near future, the higher the security we will need. The grand plan with the Internet is that all computers are connected together in a giant weblike fashion. Users can trade information and ideas, play games, and generally interact with other users they wouldn't have known existed five years ago. Everyone, at every age, can see the benefit of the Internet and use it for his or her own gain in some way. By playing games, chatting, and interacting with other kids halfway around the globe, kids can learn about distant lands and cultures. People can jump on the same connection to buy and sell stocks, research the purchase of a new home, pay bills that came in the mail, or take an online class to better their education.

Businesses that plan on attracting consumers have to not only learn about but implement secure communications from the consumer to their sites. Generally, customers don't understand the technological and political issues involved with security, but they do know when a site is looking out for the security of the customers. You must make every effort to ensure that customers feel secure. People want to see statements of security procedures and "why this site is safe" announcements. They also want to see the browser react to your site with the "padlock" or the "blue bar" indications.

The underlying problem that concerns us most is security. How secure is this technology really? Who is watching what you're doing, and how do you protect yourself from prying eyes, hackers out to do damage, or a thief interested in stealing data from your computer? In general, this isn't as big a concern as most think it is. Technology is typically invented with personal security for the user in mind from the outset. Most websites that require any type of personal information use a method of security that you can actually see. In Netscape Navigator, the bottom left-hand corner shows a small padlock either locked or unlocked, depending on the security technology of the page you are on. And in Internet Explorer, a blue bar appears just above the page content and below the HTTP location. This blue bar and padlock are indications that the site is using the Secure Sockets layer (SSL) technology. This makes the transmission of data to and from your specific machine to the server you are talking to "secure." But what does secure really mean? Enter mathematical data encryption.

SECURITY TIPS TO REMEMBER

Whenever configuring a security system, keep the following in mind:

1. Don't pick a password that someone can guess
2. Before entering your credit card, make sure you see the padlock or blue bar
3. Change your password every six months
4. Review you credit card bills to check for anything amiss.

DATA ENCRYPTION

The simplest way to protect any data that leaves your computer is via data encryption. Data encryption is the process where, by means of a mathematical formula or algorithm, data is protected because it's no longer in a format that makes any sense to the casual eye. Here is an example of how this works. Let's say you need to e-mail a confidential file to a friend. The process of data encryption ensures your data traveled to and from computers over the Internet safely. If someone does intercept your e-mail, no harm done, because only the recipient's machine has the reverse mathematical formula needed to decode the mail message. Whenever the padlock or the blue bar or Netscape Navigator or Internet Explorer, respectively, appear, data encryption is taking place.

Here's another example. Say someone wanted to transmit the letter "A" to a friend securely over the Internet using this process, here's what the sender would do. First, all keyboard keys have something called an ASCII ("ask-key") value associated with them. ACSII is the code a computer uses to actually hold and understand data. Okay, the ASCII code for an "A" is 65. The sender would take 65 and run it though a mathematical formula such as ($x * 250$), where $x = 65$. The result of 16250 is what the sender would e-mail to the friend. Knowing that the "code" to unlock the e-mail was 250, the recipient would take 16250 and divide it by 250 to get the intended message, "65." Anyone that intercepted the e-mail would just see "16250."

Of course, this is an extremely simplified description of the process; true data encryption and decryption is very complex—and very effective. In fact, it is so complex that most basic encryption applications you can buy are restricted by the U.S. government for export outside the United States for fear of reverse engineering. Even the high encryption versions of Netscape and Internet Explorer require you to register your name and address before you can download them.

The security industry is a booming business sector in the Internet world. Security is a constantly evolving concern because of the Moore's Law factor. Moore's Law dictates that every 18 months, computer processor speeds double. This means every 18 months, computers can calculate mathematical formulas faster and faster.

Data encryption relies on the fact that computers aren't fast enough to use brute-force means to calculate the data you encrypted.

To explain the concept of a *brute-force* attack, let's use breaking into a safe as an analogy here. If you know the combination, you can just apply it to the tumbler, and the safe will open with ease. In the case of a *brute-force* attack, you look at the total number of digits (let's say 100), then pick three and try to open the safe with those three numbers. If it doesn't work, you write down your failures and continue selecting and trying numbers until you get it right.

In the real world, this process would be next to impossible because our lifetime age expectancy is shorter than the number of possible solutions and the amount of time you have. However, a computer that is 500 MHz is capable of doing 500 million calculations per second—that's 500 million math calculations.

Now you should be able to see why data encryption continually evolves to try to outpace the ever-increasing speed of computers. There is no other organization in the world that leads this effort more effectively than the National Security Agency (NSA). The NSA is known as the largest employer of mathematicians currently in the United States. The mathematicians help design cipher systems that protect the integrity of electronic information systems, and they continually search for weaknesses and holes in systems and codes. All the data encryption used in banking wire transfers, for example, originated from the NSA. Even the data encrypting used in browsers has its roots in the NSA in some form or another.

SSL

Although data encryption comes in many different forms, the most commonly used is the Secure Sockets Layer (SSL) method, mentioned earlier. One reason for the popularity is that it's installed in the web browser you use already. For example, when you visit Amazon.com and log in, you are logging into a secure page that "locks" that little padlock icon in Netscape Navigator and shows you a blue bar in Internet Explorer. More than this is happening, of course. Behind the scenes, the browser you are using has negotiated something called a public-key encryption method. Your browser and the server it's talking to (in this example, Amazon.com) are transmitting and receiving data that has been first mathematically encrypted. Each computer has a common "key" to the data that is being transmitted, and no one else on the Net has that same key.

Here is an analogy of how this works. You create a little safe that only you and someone at Amazon.com know the combination to. You put your credit card number inside the little safe, close it, and spin the tumbler to lock it. You then transmit it to Amazon via the Internet, and you have no need to worry about someone seeing it as it passes by because it's locked in a safe. When Amazon gets the safe, it has the combination. Amazon can open the safe and retrieve your credit card information. If Amazon has any questions, it simply reverses the process, and you get the same safe back. (This little analogy is the part the consumer usually never "grasps"; it is meant to help you establish a mental picture of how Internet security works.) This can translate into helping you build sites that are secure and inspire consumer confidence.

Because of SSL technology, e-commerce really started to take off. Previously, people were just blindly trusting technology—until reports by the media of computer fraud began frightening people away for a period of time from using the Web. SSL is offered by a company called Verisign.com, and basically anyone can get an SSL added to its site regardless of its size or purpose. This method of security is also often used in corporate intranets where employees access a company database of information.

Overall, the protection that is offered for e-commerce is fast and effective. In addition, it has the ability to evolve and adapt to changes in the computer and technology world in real time.

A FINAL WORD ABOUT WORLD VISION

No matter which technology is eventually used for the distribution for broadband, certain global issues must be ironed out as we continue to form alliances worldwide to solidify our business position as a front-runner in the race. It is in these times that we must work together to figure out ways in which different government regulations, policies, and so forth can merge well with differing business plans and broadband strategies. As mentioned earlier in the chapter, key areas currently developing broadband technology and applications that will shape your future include Europe, Japan, and China/Hong Kong. To keep pace and to take advantage of what broadband offers, your company must look far beyond its own country and view broadband's global potential.

As a recap, following is a breakdown of the key areas:

- *Europe*—The research, development, and deployment of wireless technology here can be a model for any country. As the development infrastructure grows, we'll find better ways to deploy wireless applications, partnering up with European firms.

- *Japan*—Japan's consumer market is one that will actually take broadband e-commerce to its full potential with interactive shopping through the TV. Relationships via human-computer interaction will be more developed in this country.

- *China/Hong Kong*—With satellite and cable technology, the huge population of China will be wired with broadband.

New types of services and a brand-new market will emerge as users overseas will have exposure to your company. Hong Kong will help drive the market with STAR TV and other companies, directing content and traffic over to the mainland.

Your company must be continually aware of the developments of these areas and the many others that soon will follow suit.

Kodak and Second Story

Taking broadband further

www.kodak.com

HYPERLINK http://www.secondstory.com www.secondstory.com

"TAKE PICTURES. FURTHER."™

TAKEN ON THE ROAD: AMERICAN MILE MARKERS
MEET MATT FRONDORF

Matt Frondorf says that he's so thoroughly an engineer, he even daydreams in straight lines. So when he daydreamed about a drive across America, he saw the trip as a straight line from coast to coast.

Matt began his roadside tableau in New York City, where he framed the Statue of Liberty and shot his first photo. Then he headed west to San Francisco on as straight a line as possible, a camera at his side clicking away at precise one-mile increments, for 3,304 miles. When the camera clicked, it captured whatever happened to be on that particular American roadside—a stretch of empty highway, a street in a Midwest town, a used car lot, a herd of Herefords.

"I think I got what I hoped to get," he says. "I wanted to be able to assemble long, continuous pieces to get a feel for vastness. To look at one wheat field doesn't have the same quality as looking at the whole wheat belt."

As Matt drove through the wheat belt, he noticed that he was not the only one who thought in straight lines. Section surveyors in the 19th century had laid out a grid that produced lines of farm roads exactly one mile apart. "Just as the camera clicked, there would be a road right in the picture," he remembers. "Then another and then another. Finally it came to me that I was catching section lines exactly a mile apart. So I decided to get out of sync."

When a product company like Kodak meets a forward-thinking interactive studio such as Second Story, magic is bound to happen. For Kodak, their message of "Take Pictures. Future." has in fact furthered the notion of how technology, art, content, and community can be successfully integrated into the digital economy. Kodak is readily positioning itself as one of the leaders in the interactive broadband broadcasting business, formulating a new intelligent way to reach its customers and gain potential new ones by providing a mutually benefiting service relationship.

The American Mile Markers website (www.kodak.com/go/ontheroad) is just one of the examples of Kodak's vision for the future. Created by Portland, Oregon-based Second Story Interactive Studios (www.second-story.com), the American Mile Markers website is not your typical corporate website. "It's not advertising, it's not commerce, it's not video, and it's not brochureware," says Julie Beeler, principal at Second Story. "We believe the work represents a new form of interactive broadband programming that will become increasingly popular as more consumer-oriented companies enter the Web broadcasting business."

The site is a marvel both conceptually and aesthetically. The concept is an enriching narrative about an amateur photographer, Matt Frondorf, and the 6608 pictures he took on a cross-country drive from New York to San Francisco. The website becomes a human-interest piece, a story where an ordinary man's journey gets its chance to be told. With a camera hooked to his car's odometer, a photo on the passenger side of the car is automatically snapped every mile along the way. Whatever occurred along that stretch of road—thunderstorms over cornfields, used car lots, herds of Herefords—was captured exactly as he saw them. Visitors to this site experience Frondorf's journey in a way that would not be possible through traditional media, such as print or film. "No two experiences are the same. It's entertainment as a form of content," says Eric Rosenfeld, director of business for Second Story. The appeal of the site is widespread, garnering Kodak an audience that will consistently come back to visit the site and hopefully become loyal customers. Kodak hopes that engaging stories like these will bring users back to its site and bookmark it, allowing them to also explore the product areas of the site as well. Already the press, including *USA Today* and the *Washington Post,* has given the site great exposure by writing articles that also helped to further market the sites.

But that's not all. The American Mile Markers site is just one of 10 interactive stories that will be hosted on Kodak.com by the end of the year 2000. The stories are diverse and range across all topics of interest that could appeal to just about anyone, not just photographers and filmmakers. These elaborate stories range from the historical expedition of *The Endurance* (www.kodak.com/go/endurance) to young kids in Venice photographing the world (www.kodak.com/go/dreamteam), to cutting edge digital photographers (www.kodak.com/go/innovators), to Oscar-nominated cinematographers (www.kodak.com/go/silvergold), and finally to a living memory tribute to Martin Luther King, Jr. (www.kodak.com/go/martinluther). Beeler stresses, "We believe that eventually every major consumer-oriented company will need interactive programming—sticky content—for their Web sites. And as Broadband delivery becomes more available, audiences will expect content that takes advantage of the unique capabilities of the medium." Going forward, the broadband medium will call for more personalized, interactive content that not only is engaging but takes advantage of high-bandwidth technology, like streaming video or audio.

Because of the Web, Kodak now needs studios like Second Story and others to provide interactive digital content that will bring people to their site, keep them there, and bring them back for more. The advent of broadband distribution raises audience expectations for content by creating even more immense, informative, and engaging experiences through a dial-up connection. Kodak realizes that if they do not engage visitors by presenting fun, visually appealing, and informative programming on their website, then their audience will click away and bookmark another channel or website, perhaps even a competitor's site. Beeler believes that more than 90 percent of the people on the Internet view less than 10 percent of the websites available. How can one make sure that you are part of the 10 percent that everyone is seeing? According to Beeler, this can be done "[by] selecting sponsors and partners who can provide great distribution and exposure, selecting topics that appeal to a broad audience, and producing interactive stories and experiences that are of a level of quality and originality that they make 'top 10' lists and get linked to by portals and other sites."

This conceptual mix of one part product company, the other part service is not something new to the early adopters of broadband. Under this model, Kodak plays the role of financial sponsor, Second Story produces original content, and kodak.com is the distribution channel. By commissioning broadband human-interest content for its website, Kodak's objectives are more than simply strengthening its relationship with professional and amateur photographers. Kodak wants compelling content on its site to generate repeat audience visits, to receive recognition for being an innovative imaging company, and to create a sense of community among its customers. What is refreshing and exciting about these stories is that they are not promotional or commerce-oriented. Rather, they are human-interest stories that are designed to be entertaining and engaging and to appeal to a broad audience. Because of their interactivity, design, and multithreaded structure, these features are more than just entertaining websites. They represent an advancement of the medium.

CHAPTER 6

Changing Culture

Communications and Technology

A s has been stressed throughout this book, a fundamental change will occur in the way people communicate. We will see physical space and time break down, and businesses will be able to take on a more global scale no matter where they are located or what their size is. In this chapter, we will set the stage for what a broadband universe will look like on a very personal level, including how it affects the individual on a day-to-day basis. Then we will explore how those individual changes added to a community might impact the culture surrounding it.

One of the amazing things about the Internet is the ability to make all the players regardless of size, money, geography, or whatever seem equal. If, for example, you got a few friends together and created a website that sold book, magazines, and videos, and you delivered what you promised, what's stopping you from competing with Amazon.com? Nothing. This means that the playing field is equal and all the players are starting from ground zero. Some of the biggest companies in the world have nothing more than their company logo on there home page, while one- and two-person companies are developing outstanding sites, with rich user interactions and amazing visuals. Because the Internet is an uncharted domain, anyone with the right knowledge and patience will be able to excel there.

Jump ahead a few years when a mass number of consumers have broadband connections, devices, and cell phones. What is the impact on the culture? Is it harder to get pizza? Likely not. But technology such as broadband is really a double-edged sword because it doesn't come without an effect or consequences. But before we look at the negative and positive effects, let's examine the cause first. Done right, broadband is a way of bringing people together in a very fast and creative way. All information will be centralized into a repository we call the Internet, and the access of that information will be done via devices. This much we know. What we don't quite know is how the information will be accessed in the future—in other words, what devices and technology will be used. The ability to access the entire experience is the difference between each device. Your TV, and perhaps your computer, for example, will be used for accessing the on-demand video that the Net holds. Your cell phone might not be able to access the video-on-demand system; however, it might be able to pull up the list of shows that are in the video library to help you decide on your way home from work what you want to watch.

To illustrate the cultural effect of broadband, let's walk through a typical day in the broadband world. Then we can extrapolate that scenario into millions and see how the culture might change.

"Good morning, time to get up," your home assistant says at exactly 6:30 A.M. From the hidden speakers throughout your home, you hear the announcement "Coffee is being prepared and will be ready in four minutes." As you stumble into the bathroom, you see a blinking icon on the bathroom mirror. Touching it brings up a reminder video from your doctor to take a prescription and to make an appointment for a follow-up visit. You confirm the appointment with the touch of a button. During your shower, no real broadband potential exists—unless you are in a college dorm room and being exposed naked to the world via your showerhead webcam is something you have in mind.

Afterward, you go into the kitchen. Your coffee is perfect, and your toast has little Microsoft Windows icons burned into one side and Apple logos on the other as some humorous form of advertising. As you are eating, the toaster asks you whether you would like to try wheat toast next time. You don't reply, which is the same as a no. Walking to the refrigerator, you are presented with a menu on the door of all the contents inside—no reason to open the door and waste electricity. As you browse, you notice a few blinking items that are an indication of items that need to be replaced. With a few taps you've added those items and a few others to a delivery schedule that is expected to arrive tomorrow.

You are now ready to get dressed, and you ask your home assistant to turn on the iron and the TV. In your bedroom, the TV displays a menu of choice programs that you like to watch. You scroll through the list and pick something. Then you start ironing. The home assistant was able to activate both your TV and iron through a wireless home LAN system to which all active devices conform and respond.

After you've gotten ready and are heading out, you decide to make a few calls from your car. Your home assistant's voice is the same in your car, and simply asking her to call specific people connects you to them. In some cases, a few of the calls have video feeds associated with them, where a video image of the caller shows up on your dashboard. After you hang up, you turn on your entertainment device and are presented with all types of entertainment and information, including digital radio station broadcasts, your saved local MP3 collection, or local traffic navigation information. The commercials that are being run on the station are from places that you pass on the street almost in real time. In some cases, the ads call your attention by saying things like "Hey! See that billboard up there?" and so on, referring to the exact billboard in front of you. You have the ability to talk to cars that are surrounding you, if they wish to receive and vice versa. Your car's navigation system offers up alternate routes every now and then as well.

By the time that you arrive at work, you will have already finished responding to the telephone messages that were left for you. Then you settle down to begin working. Depending on what your job is, the new broadband network may make working with coworkers 100 times faster as well. This is where the double-edge sword part comes into play. Working 100 times faster might not sound like an exciting prospect to some. The efficiency of business will increase significantly, but at what cost? What kind of unknown stress will this put on the human body, and what are the effects on society as a whole?

Enter broadband "advice" networks. With the amazing ability to stay connected to anyone at almost any time, advise networks like medical hotlines might open up. Through your HMO (health maintenance organization) or PPO (preferred provider organization), you might be offered a service that allows you to ask a real person questions in real time. ("Why does my job drive me crazy?" might be your question at any hour of the day or night.) The ability for a global advice system to grow within a broadband/wireless environment is almost a given. People will have communication devices with them all the time to access the networks and could potentially be paid to sign up and help other people out. Doctors and medical professionals could receive money from insurance companies just like a normal doctor visit. Such advice systems could help the natural growth of a culture by educating those people that seek help. And this could help keep people healthier by getting to the cause of a problem much sooner.

Similar to advice systems are chat and forums functions. Chats are generally defined as one-on-one conversations via typing, and forums take place in a virtual "room" where several people all converse at the same time. The popularity of these is enormous. Popular forums include those on AOL, the former CompuServe, and online sites such as Yahoo. A quick visit to, for instance, AOL's chat section will give you an idea of how many people there really are online at one time. AOL has hundreds of chat rooms that can each hold about 23 people, and they are always full. Hundreds upon hundreds of people go into these forums to talk with people from all over the world about everything from sex to silverware. The forum is a unique introduction to our culture and has really only been around for a few years. Yet it is one of the most popular features of being online for many people, especially families.

Families everywhere use the Internet to stay in touch and check on other family members, to see how a baby is doing, to ask how an operation went, and so on. Some families even establish websites to announce family news in newsletters or explore family genealogy. The ability of the new Net-nuclear family to remain in touch even as members grow up and leave home is having an enormous impact on the culture of a society. This impact will affect how individuals grow up in a community and how they interact with others.

Broadband will cause other cultural changes that are harder to quantify. Categories include religion and spirituality, fashion, news events, nature and environmental concerns, and crime, to name a few. Each one of these will be inadvertently changed by the introduction of this type of global communication unification network that we are building.

In part, the impact on religion and spirituality concerns the area of artificial intelligence. What are the ramifications of a computer that is intelligent? Does it have a "soul" and no body? Although this might sound far-fetched, the Internet holds the answers to just about anything we can think of and computers that are smart enough to use it as a repository of information would in essence be modeled in the same fashion as the human brain. The first noticeable step toward this will be in the fashion of agents. Agents will be like digital assistants that you control and own and that work for you in the digital world. Your assistant could be told to reserve tickets for you that are within a specific price range or to go grocery shopping for you.

LIFTING COMMUNICATION BARRIERS

Broadband networks also offer new opportunities to people with disabilities, connecting them to the world like never before. Even if leaving their homes is physically difficult or not possible, they could go to work, to the movies, even to another country, all by using a broadband connection and a computer. Also, the high-speed connection could offer assistance to them, such as language translation or medical help through the advice system described earlier in the chapter. This could bring the minds of these people to places their bodies could not necessarily take them before.

Another perhaps unexpected potential benefit of enhanced communication concerns the area of crime. Regardless of where we live, violence is something that is close to us all. Violence is a result of a breakdown in communication. With a global broadband network in place, and some creative technology connecting the world, together we could help alleviate it. The best way violence is headed off before it starts is through education. And global education is what a broadband network could offer the youth of today. Schools could become wired, then be wired together, and then eventually be wired to universities and larger warehouses of data knowledge. Children with exceptional talents could be recognized by a computer, and a broadband connection to other schools could offer that child new course material. Classrooms could still be set up to ensure that the children matured with one another by keeping like ages together, but each child could develop at his or her own pace. A teacher would be present to make sure that each child is doing his or her work and could be offered an electronic teacher's guide that is individual for each student's needs. All of this could happen with a broadband infrastructure in place.

One of the most obvious communication barriers is the lack of money. Many people have already discovered that you can talk to another person via the Internet anywhere in the world for free. All that is necessary is a local connection to the Internet by both parties regardless of where they are on the globe and a device that connects you to the Internet (although the cost of the device itself would remain a barrier to some.) You could be driving in your car in San Francisco and talking on a wireless phone, for an unlimited time, to someone who is in Africa riding an elephant on safari. All for no more money than the local connection fee you pay to connect to the Internet in San Francisco.

Using the Internet to make global calls could provide completely free forms of voice communication to anyone. If you enabled this type of connection into a kiosk-type of device, and that device was publicly accessible, then people could stay in touch for free. No charges would be incurred other than having to watch the advertisements of products and services that appear on screen as you talk to your friends in Austria.

SPACE AND TIME MEAN NOTHING

Obviously, the distance between where you are and where you are going is defined as space. Yet this only applies in the physical world and not in the Internet world. Distance means nothing to Internet communications. You could download a file from Japan just as fast as from across the street. Regardless of how far away someone is, in a perfect broadband world, we will be able to stay in touch just as easily as making a local phone call.

Global communication devices are already here, but they rely on satellites for their signal. Because of the high technology involved, calls on such devices are currently about $7 dollars per minute—albeit from anywhere on the globe. With a wireless broadband device, however, all you need is a local wireless carrier like a cellular provider. With this device, you can then simply connect to the Net and place your call.

Your business will be available 24 hours a day to your customer, so time becomes less of a hindrance. Your customers will be able to buy from your site via their computer, cell phone, or from their PDA at any time and in any place. You should make sure that when you are designing and building your site, you take all connection devices into consideration. If you develop only for the Web, then your site is only useful for computer users. Your site must be tailored with users in mind, providing them with a rich web experience. For example, perhaps your site shows movie trailers and shorts. These would obviously be for the web browser crowd.

If we look back 20 or 30 years ago at travel and communication, we can easily see the advantage that broadband connections will offer. Years ago, going on a trip meant that you were out of touch for a long time with people you cared about. Now there are cell phones, phones on the plane, video conferencing abilities in airports, and modem lines in hotel.

Furthermore, the upcoming wireless broadband will allow you to stay in touch like never before. AT&T has currently announced a fixed wireless broadband system for completing the last mile. Although at this writing the system is only for home users, AT&T has plans for a portable device. The days of a portable DSL-type connection are coming, and it is then that space and time will really start to break down.

NEW COMMUNICATION TECHNOLOGIES AND ADVANCED APPLICATIONS

As new high-speed networks start appearing, so will a host of new communication tools. At first, we will simply see the hybridization of current devices with broadband connections. A cell phone with a broadband connection will introduce wireless high-speed communication devices that allow web surfing as well. The standard PDA, such as today's popular Palm VIII, will be wireless in the future and will offer a host of new features. In fact, the Palm VIII currently offers a connection to the Internet via a cellular-style network. With it you can send and receive e-mails, connect to specific Palm-enabled sites, and sync-up data to remote databases. Palm, Inc. has also announced that it plans on having its entire line of PDAs 100 percent wireless by the end of 2001.

Other vendors are following the lead of hybridization with their devices as well, but no one has specifically come out with a new communication device that takes advantage of broadband networks yet. Whatever these devices are called, they will all do pretty much what all the other devices already out there do, with one major exception—speed. With speed comes other features, for example, color. Sending data that contains color information can take more bandwidth than a black-and-white picture or simple text data.

Since these advanced communication devices do not yet exist, the only way to discuss them and their potential is to break down what types of services could be offered. These would include three basic types: conversational, messaging, and retrieval. Conversational services typically are a way of offering bidirectional (full-duplex) communication with real time (i.e., no storage) end-to-end information exchange from one person to another. The basic examples of broadband conversational services are video telephony, video conferencing, and high-speed data transmission.

Messaging services offer the same type of person-to-person communication, except storage units with the ability to handle data in "mailbox"-type formats would be included. Information can be stored by one user and retrieved by another. Examples of this are voice mail systems, data storage system like e-mail servers, and FTP applications. Retrieval services include data storage systems that are publicly accessible. The obvious example of this is a website. Any type of service that you put on a computer that is then open to the public for digital inspection is a retrieval system.

As discussed in earlier chapters, ATM networks are a new advanced technology on which broadband networks are being based. The ATM network has many advantages over other types of networks. ATM networks are excellent for broadband because they can adopt and change in real time to whatever the data being transmitted has to offer. In a typical office network environment, only Internet data can travel through the cabling; however, in a broadband network, you could potentially have Internet data, telephone communication, home appliances data, cable television transmission, and so on.

The ability for ATM-type networks to handle different types of traffic are what makes them unique. But what makes this capability possible? ATM can do this for many different reasons, but here are the basics.

The first is *constant bit rate* (CBR). CBR service is intended for all real-time application needs. The applications for this type of service are mainly in the voice and video area and include interactive video (such as video conferencing and video chatting), interactive audio (such as a telephone or voice chat room), video distribution (television, education, security), audio distribution (radio stations and other audio feeds), video retrieval (for pay-per-view-type events and video-on-demand services), and audio retrieval (for music libraries and voice message libraries). Another advancement of ATM is the *real-time variable bit rate services,* known as rt-VBR, which is similar to the CBR service, except that during its transmission, the data size over time can fluctuate based on the data content. This means that the bandwidth requirements can vary in real time with the content that is being sent. This method can save bandwidth for other connected users.

There are other advancements of variations that are worth mentioning without detailed description, including *non-real-time variable bit rate* (nrt-VBR), *unspecified bit rate* (UBR), and *available bit rate* (ABR). All of these make up the complete transmission advantage that a broadband ATM network has hiding inside it.

Like cable television and other telephone networks, the Internet was originally designed from the ground up with specific intentions in the minds of the engineers. That vision has truly been changed by the consumer over the years, but what about the network itself? Thanks to the introduction of smart Web browsers like Internet Explorer and Netscape Navigator, the ease of network problems has been somewhat alleviated. Both browsers have the ability to map the file you are trying to download to the application that is required to open it. It was the advent of these powerful browsers that gave people grand visions of an all-encompassing unified Web. But behind the scenes, that all-encompassing Web had some serious catching up to do. When you started to play audio over the Internet a few years back, it didn't sound any better, and in most cases sounded worse, than a telephone—not to mention what video looked like. Yet people demanded these types of services. Because the inherent nature of the Internet involves access delays (there's a reason the WWW has been nicknamed the "World Wide Wait"), downloading videos and audio clips remains a painfully slow process for most users, and this slowness of the Internet is repelling future users. With the introduction of broadband Internet connections like DSL and cable modems, the Internet can start to grow again as it did when it first became popular a few years ago.

There is one roadblock that is worth talking about, however. The quality of one network is not the same as another. The entire Internet is based on the stringing together of a bunch of little networks. If you have a high-speed broadband connection from your house to your local provider, it's not going to do you much good if the information that you are trying to access is behind the walls of a very slow network. This will make your connection feel just as slow as the slowest network in the connection. As the saying goes, "a chain is only as strong as it's weakest link," and a slow network is the weakest link here.

What can be done? Well, unless you personally own a network of access lines and want to pay to upgrade them to high-speed fiber optics, nothing. Individuals are at the mercy of others in this area. There are committees such as the Internet 2 community that has this problem in mind. As they devise plans to help build the next super Internet for the coming 20 years, the community will look at the service quality of each network and try to figure out a way to digitally label them by quality. If you have a high-speed line like DSL then you should never have to be routed through an access line.

WIRELESS/FIBER OPTICS

As we've touched on previously, it will really be the wireless connections which are offered to people which will make the greatest cultural change. Just think of the day when you don't have to plug in your computer to any wire to get high-speed Internet access. The potential for not only working from home but from anywhere in the world is enormous.

People will be able to work from home or from the road and, if need be, from vacation (although that last bit might not sound particularly desirable). Nonetheless, the ability of people to move and be connected from anywhere will be a major convenience. Spouses can easily stay connected when one has to travel on a business trip. With a video feed and a laptop computer, family members who are unable to attend in person could watch real-time events such as school plays or baseball playoffs.

As mentioned earlier, fiber optics is a communication technology with enormous potential. Fiber offers almost unlimited bandwidth and is used by every telecommunications company in the United States. The high-speed connection that you might be accustomed to in your office exists because of fiber optics. This technology is small, flexible, and easy to install. However, the home user has yet to benefit because of the giant investment telecom companies already have in the copper wire strung throughout homes.

Fiber has been deployed as test trials to a few homes in Japan and the United States, but the cost of installation, splicing, and maintenance was prohibitive. The future is still fiber, though. Once the market share increases for DSL and cable modems, the consumers will demand more bandwidth. However, just as the 56-kbps modem was the highest speed available over your phone line when it was analog, DSL and cable modems have a maximum speed too. When enough consumers feel that DSL and cable is too slow, then the next step is to install fiber optics in the home.

SMART DEVICES

Simple appliances like your kitchen blender will be Internet-enabled whereby you can monitor and control them remotely or have them all work together in a network. The whole idea conjures up images of the scene in *Pee Wee's Big Adventure* where his kitchen is automatically preparing his breakfast before he gets up by flipping stuff from one device to the other, cracking eggs, pouring milk, and so on. The result is a giant bowl of cereal filled with a quart of milk, a stack of gigantic pancakes,, and about 30 pieces of sausage. He takes two bites of the cereal, makes the pancakes talk back to him, then tosses the whole mess in the garbage. Does convenience create laziness, which in turn makes us more wasteful? Maybe so, but the potential of smart devices stretches beyond mere convenience.

In fact, the general idea based around smart devices is efficiency, and the conservation of energy is an integral part. Having one smart device in your home might not prove to be so dramatic, but when you have a houseful of devices that all can be controlled by you from a remote location the difference is obvious. Moreover, when you have more than one device, they might be able to interact with one another, one controlling and altering the aspects of the other. For example, when you hit the snooze button on your alarm clock, your automatic coffeepot, your toaster, and your television show recorder are all informed to add 15 minutes to their schedule before starting their normal cycle.

Smart devices offer the consumer behind-the-scenes benefits as well. When a smart device has problems, it can run a self-diagnosis and inform you of the results via the Web, e-mail, or if the problem is more serious, the device could contact the manufacturer and request instruction on how to correct its situation. If the manufacturer determines that the device is at fault and needs to be repaired, they might send you a new one in the mail as a replacement before you even noticed the motor in the blender was going bad. If the size of the device makes this impractical, the manufacturer could dispatch a repairperson. That person would contact you to set up an appointment and that could be your first indication that something was even wrong.

WAITING FOR YOUR INTERNET TOASTER

Broadband will slowly change the way we interact with one another worldwide. In addition, the way people shop for consumer goods and services is going to dramatically change. This opens all types of opportunities for businesses to grab the attention of the consumer. High-speed connections at home mean more than just fast downloading; they will change the way the consumer can interact with the Internet altogether. The connection is just the potential. What businesses decide to do with it is where the reward for the consumer and for businesses really lies.

The Internet-enabled toasters, blenders, and other devices don't exist yet. You can't buy them at your local Circuit City. And why not? Because your company hasn't built them yet! The consumer is ready for devices like this, the broadband network is up and working, and Internet programmers can program your idea for you. The potential is there. You just need to see it and take advantage of it.

TBWA/Chiat/Day

Building brands for the broadband generation

www.chiatday.com

TBWA/CHIAT/DAY

"Yo quiero Taco Bell." "Think Different." "It keeps going and going..." If it's catchy, ingenious, and is in your opinion one of the best TV commercials you've ever seen, it would be a good bet that the ad you love is a product of the creative genius of advertising agency, TBWA/Chiat/Day. With such top-notch clients as Taco Bell, Apple, Energizer, ABC, Levi's, and Nike (the list goes on and on), simply put, the creative minds at Chiat Day are in the business of building brands. Known for their progressive way of thinking, TBWA/Chiat/Day is already using the concepts of broadband technology today to research the future, where they can empower clients and further inspire audiences.

How would you like to start your business day with a pink slip on your desk? That's just how the people at TBWA/Chiat/Day started their workday one morning, with everyone getting "fired." The reason? It was the beginning of Reboot Camp, an internal company Internet get-together in October 1999, where 800 employees were to learn the ins and outs of the interactive world and how to go about integrating them into their advertising work. The agency is currently reinforcing the notion that to have a complete advertising strategy, an Internet and broadband strategy will be a major component to all business success. Therefore, employees had to earn their right to their job. The pink slips were ". . . a way to jar everyone into the right frame of mind for the week," recalls U.S. Account Director Sean Hardwick. "[To] learn how marketing is changing or risk being a dinosaur. A dinosaur without a job, in fact."

The weeklong event allowed employees a chance to immerse themselves in the medium. Reboot Camp featured introductions to the basics of digital media, which not only included information on the latest technologies but a briefing on who the major players and thinkers in the market are. The event also featured a trade show where companies like AOL showed off their technologies. Employees also had to rewrite their job descriptions. Hardwick remembers how Reboot Week changed his life. "It told me that the agency was serious about each one of us understanding how important and fundamental the shift in marketing has become. There was precious little hyperbole and tons of action, learning and sharing. I was left more educated, more motivated, and with more marketing tools in my toolbox."

The result? Since so many of the agency's clients were asking about interactive work, for each client an account director is tasked with bringing both interactive ideas and strategies to the table and presenting them to the client whether or not they are looking for interactive work. Dubbed "digital ambassadors," at least 1 of the 70 of these directors makes sure that clients take into account the opportunities afforded by the Internet to build their brand. The idea is that in this new dawn of the information age, Internet and broadband strategies are in fact going to play a major part of an overall brand and advertising strategy. Because so much of the agency's work is tied to building brands, developing strategies that relate to the physical as well as digital world seemed to just make sense. And because TBWA/Chiat/Day has a hand in a company's overall brand strategy, it can leverage offline media to promote online media.

More recently, on the Infiniti account, the Web was used to introduce Infiniti's new i30 luxury automobile by creating a promotional stock-picking game. The winner of the game would receive the car as a prize. An Infiniti-branded stock ticker was created by the agency, which users could in turn download to their computers.

Working in the online world, however, meant a whole new realm of deadlines. Ad campaigns that would normally take more time to produce needed to happen in a matter of hours, days, and weeks online. But to the people of TBWA/Chiat/Day, working harder, smarter, and faster is the nature of the business. "One story I love is [another ad] agency who got the computer client and told them it would take four months to produce a magazine ad," Hardwick exclaims. "The client responded by saying 'It only takes me two months to design, manufacture, and distribute the computer. So four months is a bit luxurious, isn't it?' "

Whereas web advertising today lacks punch, the web advertising of the future will end up being a mix of media—taking the best of both the online and offline worlds. TBWA/Chiat/Day knows that broadband technology is important to their clients, and they are looking at ways in which the technology can enhance the brand. "As a medium to deliver our message, we view it like the early days of cable television: not too many homes, but it will be huge in the future. Therefore, we need to learn about it today," says Hardwick. Hardwick currently sees the direction of the Web migrate toward video, obtaining valuable insight to other ads through sites such as Ad Critic (www.adcritic.com) and movie trailer previews at Apple's QuickTime (www.quicktime.com).

As challenging as it is to develop strategies for such a new medium, TBWA/Chiat/Day is working with today's online world of the

Web, as well as forecasting what to expect in the broadband future. "Less text and more video will truly allow for the medium to blossom," states Hardwick. "[E-commerce] will never be what people thought it would be, but it will see a resurgence when everyone has DSL or cable modem to download video versions of products they are interested in buying." What about business in a broadband world? With a bit of advertising wit, Hardwick adds, "[Video mail] will replace e-mail. It's much easier for an executive to speak into a Webphone/camera than type a detailed e-mail. And there will be a video record of their conversation. Airlines should worry just a bit."

Let the killer work begin.

CHAPTER 7

The Changing Culture

Commerce

The concept of shopping as a form of social interaction has been around for thousands of years. From the marketplaces of ancient Egypt to today's crowded malls where chatty teens hang out, shopping has always been something more than just the exchange of goods and services. It's another way in which consumers can be the social creatures they are.

That said, it is already interesting how the exchange of goods and services has taken on some of those social attributes as we redefine the notion of commerce into this technology-laden realm of the Internet, and now in the broadband era as it is fast approaching. One of the top auction sites on the Web, eBay, has not only provided a flea-market forum for people to buy and sell goods, but has also created a social interactive network.

There will, of course, be a balance of technology and the real world. Real, physical stores won't die and go away. With broadband, these types of physical experiences can be enhanced. Network connectivity solutions will tap into creating environments in which stores will be able to offer selection, customized product, or have customer wish lists available on hand for ease of use. The great benefit is that these two worlds will evolve and enhance each other just by the nature of competition.

Similarly, the world of e-commerce is changing. It will not matter where you shop anymore, because the technology, whether physical store or hand-held device, will depend on the consumers' convenience and their needs at that moment. The new models of shopping that created the standards for e-commerce, like Amazon.com and eBay, will find new challenges as they begin to compete with sites that merge new forms of community, higher interactive multimedia capabilities such as video, and new advertising models through content partners as well as streaming video. File size won't be an issue anymore online, and the sky will be the limit in terms of getting your best ideas in front of your customers.

THE PHYSICAL WORLD IS HERE TO STAY

So many people tout how much online shopping will take over these so-called archaic brick-and-mortar-type stores. How dare these stores think they can compete in this digital environment and future we are creating online!

It seems like almost every article about e-commerce or online shopping pits the brick and mortar stores against their hip, tech-savvy, online equivalent. For the most part, the hypocrisy lies in the fact that in reality we all live in a physical world, and the physical experience of daily life will never go away. These two models of commerce will learn from each other, both incorporating important attributes that will attract new customers, keep existing ones, and increase profits.

What comes to mind when you think of the Nike store? Cool. Slick. Cutting edge. Why is this? It's just a store, right? Stores like Nike create visual experiences so you feel like you're walking into an MTV video or one of their slam-dunk TV commercials. Video montage screens line the huge walls, employees are equipped with futuristic headsets, and interactive kiosks line up right next to the latest running shoe.

Is all this sensory overload necessary? In some ways, yes. With this techno-driven world and MTV culture on TV sets across the country, both consumers and working professionals have grown accustomed to multitasking. If you aren't on your cell phone talking while walking to your car, you're writing a proposal on your laptop, while your browser is checking for new mail. All the while the stock ticker applet on your desktop is reporting to you every quote in your portfolio, and Yahoo! is running the latest search request you made. It seems that these days you just can't be doing one thing; otherwise, you're wasting your time. Does some of this sound familiar? What happens in this fast-paced lifestyle is that these things in turn infiltrate to become part of culture, our *technoculture* to be exact.

But all this technology in stores isn't just meant to be just eye candy. Sophisticated technology is transforming the way in which physical stores can create personalized goods, such as the Levi's flagship store in San Francisco, CA. (This service is also offered in various department stores throughout the country.) With Levi's Original Spin (www.levi.com/originalspin), customers are able to custom-make their own personal pairs of jeans with the assistance of a kiosk and high technology. With the kiosk, the customers select the fabric, cut, style, and any extra enhancements that are desired. In the flagship store, customers then gear up in a body suit and receive a "body scan." This measures every inch of the body, thereby guaranteeing that each pair of jeans is sure to fit precisely. The measurements and style are stored on a special bar code to make reordering easy. All your measurements are already stored in the store's database. What's great is that there are no losses in inventory or markdowns necessary. You're not mass-producing a product hoping people will like it. Essentially, you're creating only as much as is being demanded.

Greeting cards have also gone digital in the physical stores. Most Hallmark stores around the country have a kiosk so that users can create their own cards. They can choose from a variety of designs and typefaces and choose to enter in their own message. Some kiosks also link to a flower delivery service so that you can send a personalized card with any bouquet or plant you order. Grocery stores aren't necessarily customizing their food for you, but they are getting high tech as well. Some Safeway stores are already equipped with LCD monitors in front of checkout lines with special content like news, sports, and entertainment to keep you occupied, along with a few ads thrown in just in case you didn't know there was a sale on chicken soup on aisle nine. Broadband is reaching your consumer. Digital technology will become seamlessly integrated to your customers' daily lives, as well as your own life.

It will be no surprise that, like Levi's and Hallmark, more stores will create more kinds of custom-made goods in their physical space. This blurring of physical and virtual will become more apparent as online competition drives the brick-and-mortar stores to bring technology inside the physical world. Use technology to your advantage where you can, applying the concepts of personalized, customized goods in both your physical and online space. Think about how personalized services can attract more consumers (because they feel like you are creating something especially for them), as well as the more intense interactive capabilities online commerce will create with broadband.

BUT IT'S 4 A.M.
AND I WANT A PAIR OF KHAKIS

One of the most viable features and benefits of e-commerce is that for the most part the store is open 24 hours a day. So, yeah, if you can't sleep and are restless in bed at 4 A.M., you can get up and log on to the Gap (www.gap.com) and get yourself a pair of khakis.

Your customers can do the same. With broadband, though, how e-commerce is perceived will change. Customers will no longer differentiate between the selling of goods online or offline; they will think only of the general purchase of goods and services. Why? Because the medium, whether computer, TV, or hand-held device, will be just another "door" that is always open to allow them to shop.

The shopping experience on a hand-held device compared to that on your interactive TV will be different. That's okay, because the two delivery methods have two differing usage factors. People shopping on hand-held devices are more concerned with the direct immediacy of the purchase. Interactive TV ads, on the other hand, can be flashier and more engaging to lead potential buyers to make the buy. (There is more on interactive TV further on in this chapter.) The smart way you can differentiate yourself from your competitors is to start thinking about e-commerce in a new way that will take advantage of the benefits of broadband no matter what the delivery method is.

The current crop of e-commerce stores isn't expected to last for very long. The "survival of the fittest" model will apply here as more e-commerce sites fill up web addresses and seek Internet glory. Specialty online shops enter the market in the hope of catering to niche markets and providing goods that aren't readily available to people living outside metropolitan areas. Take Boo.com, for instance, a hip, athletic clothing store that was to be the first truly "global" e-commerce site. The Boo site was a perfect introduction to broadband, but its technology didn't quite work. Customers in this pre-broadband era weren't given an option to go either high-bandwidth or low-bandwidth when Boo first launched. The site also alienated the Macintosh market, saying that the site performed better on a PC. With millions of marketing dollars spent in advertising in high-fashion and style magazines, the site itself came with all the bells and whistles that could easily ring in broadband, but it lacked the informational/organizational clarity that was important for people shopping online.

One of the items to remember as you begin to plan your broadband strategy is to never alienate your customers, especially in the beginning. You'll find that you'll need to create high- and low-bandwidth areas of your site, until the last mile has been reached. But more importantly, make sure the interactive components are appropriate for the content you are trying to sell. Video that is just flashy and that has no design concept or integration into the rest of the site or your brand will be useless broadband excess. Think through the interesting features you can supply with broadband, and make sure that you first test out your ideas before the ideas get rushed into the forefront. After all, a good amount of time planning now will save you the heartaches that Boo is currently facing. Don't worry; you'll still have time.

Service websites are also on the rise and starting to blur the nature of purchasing goods online. Sites such as Kozmo (www.kozmo.com) alleviate the wait factor by delivering movies, DVDs, games, books, magazines, food, and even electronic equipment in less than one hour. However, Kozmo is currently only offered in certain cities and zip codes across the United States. True, it will be a bit difficult for you to have a warehouse in every city and staff a team of delivery people, but that won't be the case in the future of broadband. Although sites such as Kozmo are creating new business models in the Internet industry, they are also planning ahead for broadband with their own strategies for the delivery of digital goods in the future. As slow bandwidth becomes a problem of the past, companies will be looking toward delivering digital goods, saving both costs in production (people power and time spent) as well as materials.

Kozmo founder Joseph Park is already making deals with movie and music entertainment studios in the hope that his present one-hour service company is positioned to be the broadband entertainment delivery service of the future. Park has already made deals with such big names as Warner Home Video, Columbia TriStar, and Sony. Kozmo has also struck a deal with Liberty Digital, which provides interactive video service through AT&T's cable lines. Kozmo would start selling its video-on-demand service through the Liberty service straight to your TV. Additionally, digital music could be sold and downloaded straight from the site.

Both the entertainment studios and Kozmo will benefit from this partnership. By working with Kozmo, studios essentially cut out distribution costs and can send the digital product directly to the vendor, since Kozmo becomes another store for them. For Kozmo, this is beneficial because it will have fewer overhead costs to deal with, fewer delivery people needed (assuming they will still deliver physical goods such as books, magazines, and snacks), and less of a need for inventory buildup. The transformation of physical to digital goods will be one of the underlying factors of e-commerce in the broadband age.

In the same realm, everyone else is thinking like Kozmo and is trying to make deals with entertainment studios in the hope of becoming the first to provide this new digital product. Blockbuster.com has followed suit and has made a deal with MGM to give Blockbuster the right to distribute MGM's library of 4100 films over the Internet. Users could rent movies digitally and view them on their computers, TV, or whatever the future device is to be. AtomFilms (www.atomfilms.com) hopes to do the same, but rather with its own streaming independent-film-like movies. Clearly, the message is that streaming video content is another digital good that will become one of the major goods that will be distributed and sold.

MUSIC TO MY EARS

The music industry is scrambling fast to look for ways it can cash in on the MP3 sensation, especially with web-enabled applications such as Napster (www.napster.com) under a lot of fire for opening doors in the transfer of copyrighted music to users. Napster provides the "location" from which users are able to meet and trade goods. Taking a nod from movie studios, the music industry seeks to cash in on the benefits of transferring the sale of physical CDs to digital downloadable music.

Sony is currently paving the way to sell music online that can, in turn, be downloaded directly to the portable MP3 players they produce. Music lovers can visit Tower Records and Alliance Entertainment websites and pay a small sum, about the price of a current CD single, for their digital song. Revenue for the sales of downloaded music is expected to reach $227 million by 2001 and about $1 billion by the year 2004.

But aside from all the copyrighted music debate, the technology behind Napster is something we are going to see more of. Omitting the web browser, Napster is like a self-running application, except that it takes its data from the Web. Building on this technology can enable a different kind of dynamic experience that previously was limited in many ways. We'll see a transition into more elegant or seamless interfaces that do away with the actual web browser. With Napster's technical ability, the varied search functions could enable the furthering of goods and services over the Web, where it can take on more multimedia and TV-like attributes. Besides the selling or buying of goods, and services, a network and community of users are built around common interests and can use chat/video conference features to talk about their interests or what the weather is like in Minnesota. Digital audio, along with video, will be key for any commerce- as well as content-related adopting broadband technology.

I WANT MY VIDEO!

Because the trend is a movement toward digital goods, video-on-demand will be the future of implementing interactive programming. In much the same manner that Kozmo is transitioning to be a digital goods provider, many Hollywood studios are embracing this new world of broadband, hoping to find new ways to cash in on the budding technology. The movie industry is following in the steps of the music industry, allowing for distribution on a pay-per-view basis of their films. In addition to the MGM/Blockbuster.com deal, current deals include Miramax and SightSound.com. Miramax will provide the films and SightSound will encode, encrypt, and handle the daily e-commerce transactions necessary for distributing online movies.

However, it's not just studios getting into the action. Anyone will have the opportunity to jump on the broadband bandwagon. Take Imagine Broadband, for instance. Imagine Broadband is a spin-off company out of Andersen Consulting, which is looking to make video-on-demand services available for the broadband world via the cable lines. With Imagine Broadband, cable companies could provide their technology that allows for user-specified content. While watching a movie, users could pause, rewind, and play, just like with a VCR. How this will compete with existing TV set-top box technologies such as ReplayTV and TiVO is unknown, but it will be interesting to see how they all play out in the highly competitive interactive TV market.

A report by Jupiter Communications in 1999 forecasted that the interactive TV market would reach 30 million households and become a $10 billion source in revenue by the year 2004. Interactive TV will emerge and evolve as a hybrid of the Web and TV. Couch potatoes need not worry, however. If they want to sit and just watch, they can. But those that want to be more engaged and participatory will be given the chance to do so.

There will be three main revenue-generating components to interactive TV by the year 2004:

- *Electronic program guides*—These TV schedule guides will become a staple of advertisers (as an alternative to TV commercials today) as well as of networks, which will tie in product or programming with editorial content. Reach: 55 million households.

- *Enhanced broadcasts*—Video that is interactive and "clickable" will be more engaging and will increase value and commerce ability of commercials. Reach: 24 million households.

- *Web browsing on TV*—Traditional browsing of web content with regular Internet subscriptions, advertising, and commerce usage. Reach: 13 million households.

Capitalizing on the possibilities of interactiveTV will become a challenge, because you'll have a better chance to see your advertising dollars at work. Imagine if your consumer base is the audience that watches the FOX comedy *Ally McBeal*. Presently, all you would know is the simple generalized demographics of the group and the exact time your ad will be placed. With interactive TV, your ad could be specially targeted to Jane in Los Angeles, because you know that she's a previous customer of yours and wants this new product that is coming up. Ads will be specially targeted to groups of users, and not everyone will see the same ads. The advantage in interactive TV is that while you may know that a particular episode of *Ally McBeal* garnered, say, 10 million viewers that night, you have no idea how many really saw or was influenced by your ad. With interactive TV, tracking tools will make the numbers work for you, and you will be able to find out which people viewed your ad and followed through directly with a purchase.

ONLINE GAMING

While the vision of the old video arcades and prepubescent 11-year-old boys may come to mind when thinking about video games, it's time to change that old perception today. With millions of dollars worth of revenue a year, video games have gotten more sophisticated as technology has improved. In addition, as competition gets more intense, gaming companies are currently trying to lead the way in the adoption of broadband by incorporating online gaming technology and ISP service all in one.

Both the top two gaming companies, Sega's Dreamcast and Sony's PlayStation 2, are readying themselves for the broadband world. Sega's Dreamcast console comes free with a two-year subscription to Sega's high-bandwidth ISP connection. The console will not only allow users to compete with other players who are logged into the broadband network, it will also offer Internet functions such as e-mail. The company has partnered with MP3.com to allow users to download music onto its Dreamcast devices. Launched from a new subsidiary as Sega.com, the venture is promising new monthly revenues from users, rather than relying on users to buy games periodically.

Providing a service that matches their product is the key to entering the broadband marketplace. PlayStation 2 from Sony is no different. Sony has launched a dedicated PlayStation site, PlayStation.com, that will become the primary source for PlayStation games and peripherals. The site will also offer music CDs and DVDs. The PlayStation 2 console itself will plug into either phone lines or cable for online gaming possibilities.

With these video game consoles becoming another link to TV and broadband capabilities, you'll find that there will be interesting and oftentimes very unique ways in which you can take advantage of this new medium. Special advertising on video game networks where the advertising model will be much like interactive TV can apply here as well. Sponsorships for certain gaming areas or activities can also be a new way to advertise and market yourself.

DELIVERY WILL BE EVERYWHERE

Through the integration of broadband technology in hand-held devices, video game consoles, interactive TV, and also the computer, the ability for broadband to reach the masses is insurmountable. Think about the ways in which each method of delivery can benefit your business. With this in mind, let's recap the different ways in which you can approach commerce in the broadband age.

- *Physical stores versus online stores*—Technology will play a major role in both, with both physical and online entities borrowing and adapting models from each other.
- *Hand-held devices*—Shopping in your hand will foster a different kind of experience, one that is less about browsing and more about the immediacy of the purchase.
- *Video-on-demand*—The transformation of physical video to downloadable digital goods will become one of the major components of e-commerce in the broadband age.
- *Digital music*—Similarly, the transformation of music to its digital state that is bought and sold will become another propellant of broadband e-commerce.
- *Interactive TV*—Interactive TV will be the hybrid of the Internet and your TV today. Advertising and programming models will change to adapt to this new medium, where consumer habits will be more easily tracked and purchases can be made directly from TV.
- *Online gaming*—The online gaming market will contribute to a higher growth and adoption rate of broadband access. Gaming services in turn will provide companies with a

targeted way to advertise on their networks through interactive ads or sponsorships.

In addition to the preceding ways to either distribute, sell, or advertise in the broadband age, each of these points will also fuel the adoption rate of broadband to the masses. You'll find that they will work hand in hand with each other, with the delivery method determining the way in which the digital goods and advertising are disseminated.

shockwave.com

The new Hollywood: redefining entertainment on the Web

www.shockwave.com

Remember when blinking text was the closest thing to multimedia on the Web? Then in 1995 came Shockwave from the San Francisco–based software company Macromedia. Initially, Shockwave helped transition the teetering CD-ROM market onto the Web by allowing developers the ability to use the company's star product Director in order to produce content online. However, Shockwave did a little more than help transition the CD-ROM industry; it revolutionized the Web itself. If you haven't heard or seen Shockwave by now, then you may have been living on a desert island for the last few years. The cutting-edge Web Player technology has amassed a following, and since its debut, Macromedia has also added Flash to its roster. And currently the numbers don't lie. The Shockwave and Flash players are the tops on the Web, where over 255 million users have downloaded the players and can now see Shockwave and Flash content. You'd think with all this success, Macromedia would want to take a little break. Think again. Instead, Macromedia has paved a way for yet another revolution on the Web—Shockwave.com.

As a spin-off company of Macromedia, Shockwave.com currently leads the way for the future of media broadband convergence. Filled with hip, youthful energy with original content from the likes of Trey Parker and Matt Stone's *South Park* to the comic genius of Spiderman's creator Stan Lee and his original series *The 7th Portal*, Shockwave.com is set to become the leading entertainment site on the Web. Please don't compare it to TV. Shockwave.com is producing original, interactive content that will bring entertainment to the Web. From interactive games (our favorite is the classic Tetris), online greeting cards, music, as well as a host of online cartoons, Shockwave.com is, simply put, a cool place to be. Banking not only on the successful technology created by its parent company Macromedia, and the near ubiquity of the Shockwave and Flash Players, it's actually the big Hollywood deals Shockwave.com is currently making that will make it a key player in the upcoming entertainment industry.

"Shockwave content is driving a lot of the end-user demand for Broadband," said Rob Burgess, chairman and CEO of Macromedia and Shockwave.com. "For us, the more bandwidth, the better." As an advocate of broadband, the site is not only pushing the Web further with original, interactive content, it's also helping to redefine media in this dawning era of convergence. Content partners such as Parker and Stone, as well as Hollywood luminaries such as David Lynch (*Twin Peaks, Blue Velvet*) and Tim Burton (*Beetlejuice, Batman*), have all signed "long-term participation" deals with Shockwave.com that would give Shockwave.com a piece of the pie should any of their web characters and stories spin off and garner film deals. And studios are fine with that. Not too shabby for the likes of Multimedia Gulch.

Burgess realizes that broadband is opening the doors for a new business model. Who would have thought that the Web would eventually become a heavyweight mass-media player enabling rich interactive web content to become not only a star on the Web, but potentially a star in the movies as well? As Charlton Heston once said, "Soylent green is made out of PEOPLE!" and in Shockwave.com's case, people are definitely flocking to the site. With 35 million people visiting the site each month, a roster of 15 million registered users, and new users signing up at the rate of 80,000 per day, Shockwave.com is doing all right paving the way for broadband—a high member base, original content, and interactivity that would keep anybody busy for a long time. "They are the viewing pioneers for the future evolution of the Web medium," states Eric Wittman, senior product manager for Flash. "Technologies such as Macromedia Flash, which are enabling streaming, high-quality experiences over all-bandwidth connections today, are seen as a key building block for efficient content across all platforms of the future."

Of course, Burgess' advantage is that he is CEO of both Macromedia, the software company that develops the tools and the Web Player technologies, and Shockwave.com, the destination for interactive entertainment on the Web. Therefore, the two companies really do work together hand in hand, with Macromedia driving new users to Shockwave.com from their Shockwave Download Center; and Shockwave.com in turn promoting Macromedia by showing the cool things that are being done by the company's top Web software tools. The notion here is that in a broadband world, you've got to have content to support your message. In Shockwave.com's case, the content is just a bit edgier, wackier, and more entertaining than anything else we've seen. Shockwave.com has essentially created their own broadband entertainment business model at a time when skeptics said that entertainment would never go far on the Web. So don't be surprised the next time you go to the movies and the Shockwave logo appears, eventually becoming as much of a figurehead in Hollywood as the MGM roaring lion.

PART THREE

The Changing Landscape

How Broadband Will Affect Your Company

CHAPTER 8

The New Business Networks

B ecause broadband technology affects us on a social and cultural level, realize that this kind of interaction will be most likely developed and refined by the ways in which businesses conduct their work in the next few years. Yes, you can be a key player; it's still early in the game. However, the fiber optics are reaching their last mile, and for the most part, you will want to have your business ready by the time it reaches the last house. Right now, standards are ready to be defined, and with a little ingenuity and good timing, you can be ready to put your business ahead of the crowd. Whether you have an online or offline company makes no difference. Everything that happens in the next few years will help define the adoption methods, practices, and processes that we will use to build a foundation for the future business working environment.

It is the early adopters who will be in the best position to tailor their business methods and technology to be standardized for use across the board. Think about why we use search engines/portals such as Yahoo!. This search engine may or may not be the best and most efficient way to search for items, but it has become a standard all of us have become familiar with to search for items. For the most part, people like to use things with which they are familiar. Yahoo! has become a foundation on which future models of search engines/portals can be based. Whether Yahoo! develops them or not, Yahoo! or others can elaborate on these models.

Translating that into your business means a few things. First, you can begin your broadband strategy and vision by starting internally within your office. How can you improve the internal workflow and process? Most offices are already in the early stages of broadband, with fast company networks in place. By communicating through high-bandwidth networks within the confines of the company's firewall, you are in an ideal position to identify ways of transmitting fast data and to reap the benefits by applying this technology to your office environment.. To help make the full emergence of broadband happen, you will need to take advantage of its greatest attribute—its speed.

Broadband will allow for efficiency in the workplace. From tasks such as transactions or approvals online to video conferencing in your next meeting, you'll be able to work faster and smarter. Additionally, the rapidly growing business-to-business e-commerce industry is the next speed that will help you keep costs down and bring efficiency to the workplace.

Don't worry, we aren't forgetting about one of your most important assets—your customer base and the potential reach to new customers. The changing nature of the consumer market due to broadband will be an integral part of your company's broadband vision and will determine how you can approach customers in the future.

INTRANETS—BROADBAND STARTS WITH YOUR OFFICE

Another way to take advantage of the broadband in your office is by using the internal network of your company to its full potential.

Through intranets or extranets, you will be able to create efficiency in terms of consolidating all company documents in one place. These networks can also become an efficient way to manage projects internally or with your clients.

Take the entertainment industry, for instance. With such large studios and the sheer volume of shows being produced, making sure that the process and flow for approvals is efficient can be quite difficult, especially with shows produced by multiple studios. Production for the WB network show *Felicity* found an efficient way to coordinate cohesive branding through the use of a Web-based extranet (extranet here because it is shared between three external companies) created by Culver City, California-based Hello Design. Imagine Entertainment, WB, and Disney essentially share the show. The objective was to create a focal point for the various companies and individuals involved in developing and promoting the show. The result was a site that managed efficiency and created a center that consolidated most of the approval process.

The *Felicity* extranet helps connect staff.

Visual search functions that quickly download or order an archive of Felicity images, an organized searchable archive of Felicity merchandise, and creative brand guidelines allow a manner in which collateral can be expanded to allot for archiving and growth potential. The site also became an efficient content management tool for posting samples of artwork awaiting approval, which could be done directly online. Functions that used to take days can now be done in minutes. The workflow is streamlined, because users can get answers to their questions just by logging on. With hectic schedules, users can now also contribute to key decision-making processes at their own convenience from anywhere in the world. Taking advantage of high-bandwidth networks in the business world is the first step to efficiency and will soon be the major method to use in running your business internally.

B-TO-B: BROADBAND ACROSS BUSINESSES

While at work, don't you wish sometimes you could clone yourself when it comes time for the mundane tasks? You know in your heart that these tasks are important, but a part of you would rather concentrate your efforts on more important matters, like new business, projects, or perhaps the meaning of life. True, there have been a few successful cloning experiments with a couple of animals, but let's be realistic here. A better alternative to those work woes is the new wave of business-to-business, or B-to-B, commerce that is, jump-starting the broadband revolution.

According to a Forrester Research study in February 2000 based on interviews from Fortune 1000 companies, 93 percent of firms expect some aspect of their business trade to flow over the Internet by the year 2002. Combine that with the fact that more than $1.4 trillion will flow though online markets by the year 2004, and it all gets very exciting. As you can see, an enormous shift is underway.

Whether your business is a high-tech Internet startup, a construction company, or even a grocery store, broadband adoption in the business world will start with B-to-B commerce, as it will allow for smoother workflow in the company. Just as e-commerce flooded the Internet revolution, B-to-B networks will jump-start the broadband revolution. How will it happen? As technology advances, it is most easily adopted in its early stage in the business world—first, because they have the infrastructure internally to do so, and second, because the companies can afford to do so before the general public can. A new genre of online business commerce will introduce and educate the business world concerning how tasks can be made more efficient in the workplace. As the initial use of broadband technology becomes adopted in the workplace, technology will then adjust itself progressively for the masses.

Those mundane tasks, such as ordering supplies, filling out paperwork, or even bidding on contracts, can be automated to save time and money. No longer will employees need to go through endless supply catalogs and fill out manual requisitions. Everything that can be done online should be, in order to take advantage of saving time.

The benefits of saving time are obvious; in business, time means money. Not only are companies spending less by not having numerous superfluous employees, the end result of the savings on a macro level can translate into higher profit margins, or even become extra money that can be invested back into the company for research and development.

Cisco Systems, a maker of networking equipment, does all of its manufacturing and distribution transactions online. Because of that, the company estimates that it saves about $70 million a year. Sounds pretty good, right? The reduced cost factor also includes the fact that with a high-speed network, there is a lesser need for the number of bodies to physically do the work. Much like the efficiency created by the introduction of the assembly line in the automotive industry, B-to-B commerce instead will foster a virtual assembly line that can cross physical location and time zones. It can also allow for the possible mass customization of tasks that can make your company run like clockwork.

The ease of entrance to this market is large, since potentially any industry can benefit. In April 2000, six major airlines—Air France, American Airlines, British Airways, Continental Airlines, Delta Airlines, and United Airlines—invested $50 million in an online B-to-B marketplace. The service would link carriers world-wide with goods and services related to the airline industry, such as fuel and fuel services, airframes, engine components, and maintenance services. The new alliance will be a new company based in the United States and will traffic some $32 billion per year in online transactions. It was made clear that no purchases of planes would be made over the marketplace, which may be a relief to frequent flyers. Airlines will have a one-stop shop to find all their goods and services, saving valuable employee time and company overhead costs. Also, because suppliers want to compete in this new market, prices will be very low, giving airlines more savings in their pocket.

As every business begins to adopt the notion of B-to-B commerce, a business network will begin to occur. As business networks, these companies will be positioned to better compete in the marketplace. Why? They will have superior connections to the latest prices, market feedback can be instantaneous, and information on a global scale will be at their fingertips. The power has thus shifted from those that supply the goods to the buyers themselves. Because the early adopters in this arena will have an advantage over those that are not, the level of networking will grow between the companies that are competing in this marketplace and they will be the leaders in their respective fields. They will be able to define the B-to-B marketplace, as well as the future of broadband.

Because B-to-B is tied so integrally to the speed and high-bandwidth nature of broadband, essentially, business models created with B-to-B applications will find their way down to the B-to-B marketplace of the future. In addition, compared to brick-and-mortar suppliers, online B-to-B savings can be extremely high, especially since most of the transactions that are processed are at such a high volume of goods. According to research by Goldman Sachs, savings with B-to-B for electronic components is 29 to 39 percent, metals is 22 percent, life sciences is 12 to 19 percent, and computing is 11 to 20 percent. What does this mean? There will be a power play between the brick-and-mortar companies and the online companies. And with more players entering the market, prices in the B-to-B marketplace will surely get lower as companies are trying to leap ahead with their markets, trying to provide the lowest possible price.

A new breed of players in the market is the "online market-makers"—e-commerce companies that are linking buyers and sellers over the Web. Companies like Ventro, an online chemicals marketplace, and Freemarkets, a trucking services network, are excellent examples of how personalized company needs can be better tailored through online networking for lower prices on supply goods or bids on contracts. FreeMarkets uses an auction model much like eBay. However, instead of bidding on old records, suppliers use these real-time auctions to bid for contracts. These contracts added up to about $2.7 billion dollars in industrial materials for Freemarkets in 1999.

B-TO-C: BRINGING BROADBAND TO YOUR CONSUMERS

E-commerce equals Internet strategy. Some companies think that by just having a store on the Web they are connected and in tune to showcase their products and services. With broadband, businesses can redefine the way they communicate with customers and educate them about particular products and services.

E-commerce will take on interactive capabilities that will merge the video component of TV with the interactive and personalized possibilities of the Web. Sites will be immersive, interactive experiences that will also tie content into the consumer's shopping bag. But what does this mean for you? This means that in order to think ahead to the broadband capabilities of the future, you'll need to have interactive components ready for your consumers. In turn, because of improving technologies, you'll also have better tracking tools to target specific products you have to exactly the right consumer. So Sally in Michigan who likes chocolate chip cookies will see the chocolate chip ads, while Michael in California will see the oatmeal-raisin cookie ads, because those are his favorite. It's almost as if you are sitting right there in your consumers' houses, documenting their every want, their every move, and their every purchase.

Building your online brand around your community of users will also be important in the broadband world. As consumers are more technologically savvy, you'll need to create "destinations" that will allow users to communicate with you and with each other, in addition to selling your goods online. By finding creative ways to empower the consumer, companies will adopt interesting new ways to reach out to consumers when bandwidth is no longer a problem.

BEYOND THE AD BANNER: THE PROMISE OF RICH MEDIA

Can you remember the last time you clicked on an ad banner? When was the last time you even read an ad banner? As web surfers, all of us have found ways subconsciously to block out the top of the web page and go straight to what we are looking for.

How does that make you feel as you start to invest in advertising on the Web?

It's true that currently advertising on the Web has been severely limited to the boring standard horizontal 468 x 60-pixel animated GIF that is supposed to be "interactive." It's interactive because there's text that says "click here." What has happened to our society?

We were once told of an interesting conversation that could raise the blood pressure of anyone involved in a Web-centric business. It was between an acquaintance and a director-level media person at one of the top 10 most trafficked websites. While talking about rich media, the media person told the acquaintance that the file size limit for their site for all rich media content was 12 kB. He said it so matter-of-factly too. The acquaintance actually thought the media person was getting it wrong and said, "Oh no, I'm not talking about animated GIFs. I mean rich media. Do you know what rich media is?" But 12 kB it was. "What's the point of rich media if it's 12K?" the acquaintance asked. The director had no real response, just indifference. He was actually trying to steer the acquaintance away from doing rich media because of the hassles that supposedly went with it. That scared the acquaintance, as well as us, because whatever you think of as rich media now, Java or flash banners or interstitials, can really be tossed out the window. We are so crazed over file size limits today that we are forgetting about how meaningless it will mean in the broadband future. With streaming technology and the increase in bandwidth, you won't know a video is really 100 MB; you'll just know that it was a great site, perhaps selling a great product.

Cable modem service provider "broadband" companies such as Excite@Home boast that they are leading the way in interactive advertising. True, their work is the furthest thing away from a typical ad banner right now. However, businesses will need to move away from the obvious ad-banner-like real estate. Click-through rates, impressions per minute, all these measurements in the web advertising realm are models that are about to be broken down because they just don't work. Putting a file-size limit on rich media is ridiculous because, quite frankly, real interactive rich media will be the savior of advertising on the Web. As we approach a broadband world, rich media advertising will be similar to the way in which television advertising is done, but with an interactive slant. No longer will consumers be limited to small banner ads. There will be more of a blurring between content and advertising, such as full-scale interactive branding advertisements that can not only track viewers and usage but link directly to sales.

One such example is a new company called Point-Click-Purchase (www.point-click-purchase.com), which is targeting broadband audiences only. If you don't have high-speed access, please visit when you do. The company is using a TV commercial-like environment and QuickTime 4 technology to make interactive advertising and shopping a reality. So, if you're watching a Gap commercial and you like those khakis on the dancing model, all you have to do is "roll over" the khakis and click on it. Then a pop-up browser window will appear, and you can purchase the khakis from Gap.com. The site is currently in the works, since there are no deals with merchants or content providers as of yet, but it's just a matter of time before the site will garner more interest.

But suppose you are approached with a site advertising a new book by your favorite author, perhaps Stephen King? In the future, web advertising will be smarter. Knowing that you bought a Stephen King book a few months ago, it will present you only with advertising that you would be more inclined to buy.

Companies will realize that in order to advertise on the Web, they will need to have specialized experiences that will either engage users to really learn about their products or services, or engage them to meet and communicate with each other. The key words here are *interactive*, *content*, and *personalization*. Users not given the opportunity to be engaged will essentially become bored and log off.

CONTENT IS KING

So how can you think ahead to create advertising that will take the best advantage of the technology and its movement into broadband? Be creative yourself, or partner up with a content provider. That's right, finally all that Marshall McLuhan (*The Medium Is the Massage*) discourse will ring true. Content is king.For the most part, a kind of editorial/advertising that's used quite often in the magazine world can be really effective when companies begin gravitating toward broadband. Television advertising won't be these interstitial breaks that presently appear between shows. Showcasing a product with a story will be the next way in which to engage users, informing them on a subject (hobby, human-interest story, breaking news) and selling products indirectly.

And we're talking about new content, not regurgitated old video or trailers. Coming up with something fresh for the broadband audience will be a challenge, but the results can be amazing. Websites will be more like web channels producing interactive content that will do its best to engage and sell, as well as create a community of users. Currently a big site such as Nike, mentioned earlier in the chapter, doesn't just sell product with a list of links. It's creating engaging interactive stories and special sites that tie into the product. Stories or minisites, such as the Charles Barclay Network and the Lance Armstrong story, not only provide engaging material, but they also tell the users that Nike is committed to them and inspire them with tales of their favorite sports heroes.

Sometimes, your audience can create the content for you. Take the site Spotlife (www.spotlife.com), for example. As a spin-off company of Logitech, the number one maker of webcams and other peripherals, the site is hoping to build a community of online video junkies—and sell a few webcams in the process. The concept is that anyone who has a webcam will be able to stream his or her own content on the Spotlife site, thus creating an individualized "channel." It's sort of like your own web cable-access show. To promote new users to the site, Spotlife is taking a nod from the popular MTV show *The Real World*, housing seven people in the same MTV real world house on Lombard Street in San Francisco. The live nature of the webcam broadcasts gives it more of an edge over other sites that broadcast video such as AtomFilms. Sites such as Spotlife allow hardware companies such as Logitech a chance to use the interactive and two-way communication potential of broadband to their advantage.

AND NOW A WORD FROM OUR SPONSOR

Another way to reach customers is to build your brand through sponsorships. Sometimes, by sponsoring an online event or website, you can significantly increase your brand awareness. With so much of the broadband movement being jump-started by online video and special broadcast streaming events, lending your name to cutting-edge events or sites can put your company at the top. Users will recognize your efforts. A sports immersion site such as Quokka Sports (www.quokka.com) is ready for broadband, covering all angles of sports from sailing to race-car driving to mountain climbing expeditions. In addition, it has formed a joint partnership with NBC for the 2000 Olympics.

Visa also has a variety of sponsorships with various retailers, creating online advertising that will not only promote

1-800-Flowers but the use of a Visa card as well. Find out which sites or companies you would like to align your company with and inquire about sponsorship opportunities.

ENDLESS POSSIBILITIES

For the most part, looking at both B-to-B as well as B-to-C options are important as we move toward broadband. Start with your own office and company. By focusing on internal networks, you can move your company process online, creating efficiency and higher profit margins. Transactions via B-to-B networks will fuel broadband to the rest of the business world, creating an environment whereby the majority of work will take place online. The great advantage about heading into the broadband world is that everything will finally become more engaging and more creative. Be an early adopter and make sure you can make your mark with the high-speed network of the future that's fast approaching.

Columbia TriStar Interactive

Creating successful broadband strategies

www.spe.sony.com

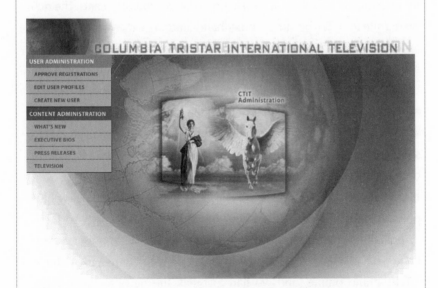

The glamour and glitz of Hollywood doesn't faze the likes of Creative Director and broadband visionary Wyndham Chow of Columbia TriStar Interactive. He's got a lot of websites to create and manage, but at the same time, he's ready to bring Sony's broadband vision to the rest of the company and the world. As Hollywood studios try to find their place in the broadband scheme of things, Columbia TriStar Interactive is already leading the way.

Columbia TriStar Interactive, or CTI, is the online marketing, promotion, and multimedia production division of Sony Pictures Digital Entertainment Group. Responsible for the award-winning online SPE! web network (www.spe.sony.com), CTI is at the center of Sony's larger broadband initiatives to bring Sony entertainment products to users through new delivery platforms with innovative and original programming. According to Chief Executive Howard Stringer of Sony Corp. America, "Sony is seeking to marshal our assets in film, TV, new media, and content creation to take a leadership position in the expanding field of broadband entertainment."

One of Chow's first forays into broadband was an extranet site that showcased Columbia TriStar International Television, CTIT, (Sony Pictures International TV distribution arm) to potential distributors/clients. The rich media site for CTIT became a broadband learning experience for Chow and his staff. The goal of the site was to create ". . . a resource for one stop marketing support where our clients can come to instantly view and download marketing materials, find out about us and upcoming events, and provide competitive intelligence to the sales field." The site uses the Web in its full broadband potential with streaming video trailers, photo stills, and one sheets (informational data sheets on the TV shows). Yet, one of the challenges Chow faced was not just with the technology, but with having to educate CTIT's clients as regards "the ever expanding wishlist phenomenon," as well as explain the nature of technology to CTIT. "Updatability, file size, transfer rates, bandwidth costs, and user-experience were all very real issues that went along with the helping to build CTIT's brand online, and we had to break the news to them rather gingerly how that formula works," says Chow.

Sophisticated back-end technology allowed the site to become the rich and robust broadband application it is today. Being database-driven, the front-end website had to tie in seamlessly with the back end. "CTIT's business is selling TV shows, not maintaining a site. So with Hello Design [a web studio based in Culver City, California; www.hellodesign.com], we developed a solution that had a very straightforward Web-based GUI [Graphical User Interface], but with a very robust backend that could swap assets out on the fly and still maintain a very consistent and elegant look and feel," recalls Chow. "In the end, Hello Design did a great job integrating the technology and coming up with a very usable GUI." Previously, Columbia TriStar International Television sent out costly promotional print and video materials that were difficult to update. With this new system, Columbia TriStar International Television is now able to effectively update and change content for their users instantly while saving both time and money.

By starting internally with a broadband strategy, Sony Pictures Digital Entertainment Group is now seeking ways to have its various departments collaborate more. "It's going to be great having Imageworks [a 3D/FX house], SOE [Sony Online Entertainment (online games)], and CTI working together," says Chow. With CTI as one of the cornerstones of Sony's overall broadband vision, bringing new forms of entertainment to a larger audience, Chow is optimistic and enjoying the new broadband direction of the company he's helping to form. "It's really exciting to be part of a company that embraces technological innovation as a core function of its business strategy. Because of this, it's not out of the question for us to partner with technology leaders to create new experiences online. We are currently working on developing authoring tools that will allow broadband users the ability to create their own content and share it with their friends. We've also been very active at creating opportunities with traditional media creatives and offering our expertise in interactive development."

CTI's broadband experience doesn't fall simply into the Web. It was the first studio to create web content for hand-held wireless devices like the Palm, as well as paving the path in interactive TV. Last fall, Enhanced

TV versions of the popular TV game shows *Jeopardy* and *Wheel of Fortune* debuted, marking a significant path in the road to convergence. Enhanced TV allows TV viewers to play along online as the game show is happening on the TV screen.

Through collaboration and extensive research of new technology, Chow has learned the ropes on what it takes to build a successful broadband application. The learning curve of the CTIT project has helped him and his team as they continue to grow and amass more experience in the broadband world. Undoubtedly, Chow is excited about the direction of all this new technology. As Chow says, "Beyond CPMs, click throughs, revenue models, and cool technology, I hope that broadband will offer better human interaction. The growth of the Web is about humankind's desire to relate to other people; to find common ground. Broadband, if done well, will be able to do this in ways not previously possible."

Innovation and creativity has helped Columbia TriStar Interactive stay on top of the broadband revolution, paving the way for how we consumers can be entertained, but also for the innovative, technologically advanced ways in which companies will communicate and function in the new broadband economy.

CHAPTER 9

The Changing Technologies

With the advent of high-speed broadband performance networks, electronic devices that better take advantage of this newfound high speed will start to emerge. At the very least, computers and devices connected to a broadband network will change to accommodate the hardware used in broadband connections. The first and most obvious is the modem or connection device. In the case of DSL, consumers and businesses can expect to start seeing computer manufacturers offering DSL modems as a preconfigured, preinstalled solution right along with the computers they are purchasing.

But what about the cable modem? It all depends on who controls the cable modem hardware and if those companies allow modems to be sold independently. Some Internet cable providers might not want to give up the control of selling modems themselves. With DSL, a third-party company such as Actel sells the modems to the local phone company or ISP provider, and the provider factors this into the cost of the installation and monthly charge. In most cases, customers are charged a one-time charge of, for example $200, then simply pay a monthly connection fee to access the Net. No per-minute or per-download charges.

Once the cable modems and DSL modem manufacturers start aggressively selling or installing their hardware, vendors of other hardware technology devices in addition to computers could start adding DSL and/or cable modem connection abilities to whatever device they want. This functionality is really what the changing of technology is about.

With the wireless Internet coming, adding wireless DSL and/or cable modem access speed to a device that is part of our everyday lives will bring about a host of new information. The way the Internet is set up now requires humans to enter all the data that we are presented with, with the exception of the webcam, where we can get information without someone ever having to enter any data. This "monitoring" ability will grow even more popular in the age of wireless communication and data flow. For example, if traffic and intersection conditions were continuously monitored and broadcast into the Internet, that data could be analyzed and used for traffic control and flow purposes. The data could be presented to the consumer in real time, and it could be accessed anywhere. If you were at home, you could quickly check the most efficient route to travel across town. If there were any accidents along the way, your onboard navigation system could warn you to deviate from your original driving plan because a more efficient direction has opened up.

With the obvious popular support behind broadband, the next logical step is the mass integration of broadband into all existing forms of technology. But what does that mean? Well, for starters a common programming language might have to emerge. Many companies have recognized this and have already started development efforts.

Bluetooth is a new technology that is being backed by Ericsson, Motorola, and Microsoft. Bluetooth networks technologies together via wireless means, so you are likely to hear about its usage in PDSs, cell phones, and mobile PCs in the near future. Another technology is the universal plug-and-play connection technology. Known as UPnP, this technology has backing from players such as 3Com, Hewlett-Packard, Maytag, GE, and IBM. The technology will allow devices to network via normal Net standards such as the HTTP and IP currently used today. In addition, Sunbeam plans to use its Home Linking Technology (HLT) to link home appliances together using standard electrical power lines as the communication link. (With this technology, for example, your bathroom scale could tell your refrigerator to stop buying food because you are overweight.) HLT is the first technology that is taking a stab at making its own home network by using the power lines that are already running through your home. Not a bad idea. The company plans on having devices for sale by late 2000.

Sun Microsystems, of course, will be a player in this area too. Because of its Java programming language, programmers have been able to write code once, then play it back on any computer platform. In adddition, Sun has a new language it is developing, named Jini, which is based on the Java language and is being backed by Sony, Cisco, Motorola, and Oracle. These developments sound very promising and powerful, and they have broadband integration written all over them. The Jini language could potentially be used in cell phones, PDSs, home appliances, printers, and other electronics. Sun promises that the Jini "layer" uses Java to connect all these devices together; and with the success of Java, we have every reason to believe them.

With all these companies developing different technologies, hopefully they won't lose site of the fact that making the world a better place to live is their mission. If simply adding technology for the sake of business is their plan, then we will inadvertently end up with technologies that make the simple things in life such as getting a glass of water much harder. However, if the complicated elements of, say, having different home electronics work together are resolved, then their mission will be successful. One such endeavor is the HAVi technology. Short for Home Audio/Video interoperability, this technology has the backing and support of companies such as Grundig AG, Hitachi, Matsushita Electric, Philips Electronics, Sharp, Sony, Thomson Multimedia, and Toshiba. HAVi technology would ensure the communication between devices such as TVs, stereos, cable modems, Internet TVs, DVD players, and so on. Anyone who has tried to assemble a home theater and didn't have all the components from the same manufacturer can easily see the benefit here, not to mention the added advantage if these devices were controllable from the Net somehow.

All this bandwidth is available in the form of broadband. Broadband-ready devices are being developed, and all of them can intercommunicate with one another. Now what? How do you as a business owner thrive in this type of environment? How do you get your message to the consumer, and how can consumers tell you what they are expecting?

REACHING THE CONSUMER

In this new Jetsons-like lifestyle, reaching the consumer is going to be tricky. Right now, web banners and web ads are the most common form of Internet advertising, next to spam, or junk e-mails. The average click-through rate of a web banner is about 2 to 3 percent. As mentioned in the previous chapter, those of us who are on the Web regularly tend to block out these banners.. This isn't to say that these banners aren't effective at all. You generally will remember a banner and what it was offering just by seeing it flash in front of you.

However, to really grab the attention of the consumer, you need to use more compelling technologies and, frankly, better ideas than Pong-like games or "catching" the item moving back and forth. A general rehashing of ideas seems to be a phenomenon surrounding people working in this area. For example, Atari came out with its first game console, the 2600, with games such as Pong and Tank, over 20 years ago. Yet the first time a new multimedia technology comes out, such as Shockwave or rich media banners, the tendency is to make Pong-, Space Invaders- and Breakout-type games all over again. Come on, someone thought of that concept 30 years ago, think of something new! Clearly, when individuals and businesses take the extra time and allow for the creation of new ideas, they can expect better results in customer response.

Just keep in mind that reaching your audience is really all about strategically placing your ads or offering them in just the right place at just the right time. And in an emerging broadband market space, where many devices and delivery methods don't yet exist, this will be a gray area at first. However, once we are settled in the age of the "active" appliance, your demographic targeting will be fairly automatic. The consumer will have a digital profile that will, unfortunately, pretty much be public information. For example, even today when you surf the Web with your web browser, sites that you visit can grab your e-mail address from the browser and use it to target you demographically based on the content of the website you have just visited. If you visit clothing sites often, you will start getting random junk e-mail that pertains to offerings that are clothing-related. Because of security concerns and safeguards built into browsers, your e-mail address is just about all they can grab and use. (You can, of course, beat them by altering your e-mail address saved in your browser's preferences.)

The digital profile, or dProfile, might sound like a scary concept, but just like the preferences hack, those who want the convenience of the device but value 100 percent privacy will figure out a way to get it. The dProfile is really a new business concept in its own right. The idea is that all of these so-called smart devices will initially need some basic input from you in order to seem smart later. And even though these devices might be collecting little pieces of information at a time from your customer, added together they create a digital profile of everything about your customers and their lifestyle. It's a scary concept that is going to start all types of regulation, security, and privacy issues. In addition, the security issues that a digital profile creates affects your customers' personal safety. Say, for example, a refrigerator has an initial setup question about the hours that its owner is at home because it wants to go into power-saving mode, and this information somehow makes its way into the hands of a criminal, they would have the best and worst times to attempt to break into the home. (Maybe it's ok, if the criminal plans to steal the refrigerator that enabled access to the house in the first place.) With such scenarios in mind, it's easy to see the need for some type of control organization or standards that define consumer privacy.

When a dProfile is generated about your customer, you can start targeting the customer specifically. It might mean an advertisement scrolling across the glass of the microwave. For instance, one company is working on a concept microwave that has a bar code scanner in it so that when a user scans an item, it cooks it for the user. That scan could have just updated the consumer's dProfile to reflect his or her enjoyment of some type of frozen dinner, suddenly featuring ads on the microwave door that correspond to the item currently being cooked. Other devices could also offer advertising in a compelling and fun manner that might not be so intrusive to your customer's life. The stereo or clock radio could scroll text ads across the LCD screen that the radio station was encoding into the broadcast signal; perhaps it would eliminate the need to run actual commercials!

While we are on the subject of creating ads to reach your customers, start thinking about the delivery methods and technologies too. As mentioned, standards and devices aren't currently in place, so a true understanding of how you are going to deliver your message with X technology isn't known. However, you can bet it will be safe to play with the current rich media delivery methods. Rich media is currently delivered with Shockwave, QuickTime, or Java.

The Shockwave technology is a delivery plug-in that supports the playback of two host applications, Macromedia Director and Macromedia Flash. Both of these applications will compile their interactive content into the Shockwave format and even write the HTML page necessary for serving it up for you. However, there are considerable differences between the two applications that are worth a brief mention here. First off, Director is more complex. The application itself is easy to use, but its interactive capabilities require the learning of a programming language called Lingo. Lingo is an extremely powerful, flexible, and fast language that could allow you to literally write Netscape Navigator in Director, then compile it into your own application. It is a serious multimedia development environment that has its roots in the interactive CD-ROM soil. Because of this extensive robust feature set, rich media advertising flexes 1 percent of Director's muscle. But in the hands of a capable developer, there is nothing that Director couldn't rapidly create.

Macromedia Flash, on the other hand, is an easy application in comparison to Director. Flash is a vector-based animation tool that is similar to Director in its "animation over time" concept, but it has only a tiny percentage of Director's interactive programming abilities. This hasn't stopped it from emerging on the Web in some very compelling interactive sites and rich media banners. Flash is a strong application for broadband because of its vector quality (think small file size) and its ease-of-use factors. At this point you might be wondering why small file size is being emphasized in this discussion of broadband.

Even in a high-speed networking environment, you will still want to use the most efficient tool to allow for the highest degree of development flexibility. Because of this, both Flash and Director are good tools to investigate.

QuickTime is Apple Computer's answer to multimedia/rich media. QuickTime is an amazing piece of technology, and few developers truly realize its full power. Most people simply think QuickTime plays those little movies they see on the Web. However, QuickTime can deliver just about any type of experience you can think of to your customer in a host of different formats and environments. QuickTime is an architecture that facilitates the delivery of video, sound, animation, text, and vector graphics. In addition to simply delivering this type of content, it can also have a layer of interactivity embedded within it. This interactive layer is at the heart of rich media delivery. Another important feature of QuickTime is the fact that it streams its content to the viewer, which allows for the immediate playback of files such as video regardless of the file size. QuickTime can automatically determine a computer's connection speed and then deliver a movie, sound, or whatever to your customers specifically tailored for their bandwidths.

Regardless of what technology you actually use to reach the consumer, your message is what really needs to be communicated. And with all the coming new broadband active appliances, media placement services will be the most effective way to match your message to the audience that you are looking to target. After all, you need to work with current media-placement companies for banner and rich media ad placement, as they will have a major stake in broadband advertising as well. The tricky part is getting them to accept the fact that a banner can now be larger than 10 KB!

With all these devices coming, you will really be able to more effectively put the message a consumer is interested in right in front of them at the right time. The refrigerator could be used to advertise produce, dairy, and other food items. The home stereo could show advertisements for music that could be purchased and possibly downloaded right into the stereo's memory for playback. The stove or microwave could be used to advertise all kinds of goods, ranging from food dishes to cooking utensils. Now think for a moment where there is glass or mirrors in your home. These items could be replaced with either some type of liquid crystal display that could be used to access information but also show ads too.

Let's move away from advertising for a moment and focus on other ways of reaching the consumer. Perhaps you want to extend to the broadband community pieces of information, or you simply want others to know you are there. What then? Well, in terms of the wireless consumer, some very exciting technology is fast approaching. Imagine you are driving in your car through a city and you are interested in knowing what's around you. You activate your car's local information system, and suddenly, you are hearing ads for places as you drive past them. Or you can request (with your voice, of course) a Chinese restaurant. You are then presented with talking advertisements from restaurants based on their proximity to your car. In order for this system to work, however, a few occurrences must happen. Local vendors, stores, or restaurants that want to be on this "public broadcasting system" need to invest in a small piece of hardware that emits information about them. The device will need to be located on the store's premises.

The trouble with this idea is that most simple storeowners may feel intimidated by this prospect, thus preventing the idea from growing. A better solution for this system to work is called triangulation, be it cellular, satellite, or GPS. The way this works is fairly simple. Picture a map in front of you with three dots on or near the edges. These dots represent the transmission and receiving antennas. Now, in the middle of this map is your car, which is emitting a request for local service information. In your mind, draw a line from each antenna to the car. This is what triangulation does. Based on the strength of your signal and the direction it is coming from, and having multiple antennas picking up that signal, your location can be pinpointed down to a dime. The system cross-checks its database for participating stores, vendors, and restaurants in you area and broadcasts the information to you. No hardware on the advertiser's part is necessary, just a monthly subscription fee.

Besides proximity broadcasting, another method for literally taking your message to the street is via kiosks. Kiosks are nothing more than public terminals that allow access to the Internet. The service could be free; recouping its cost through advertising revenue. The traditional problem with kiosks was that they would internally hold a few hundred MB of attraction data, like video loops and sound bites. However, when the consumer actually started to play with the device, there really wasn't much information there—especially if they wanted information that the kiosk had to retrieve through a phone line. The consumer ended up with a dial-up 56-kbps modem connection, and just walked away because the kiosk's connection was too slow. By connecting kiosks to a broadband network, you could eliminate a few problems. First, the kiosk wouldn't need to locally store its attract loops and sound bites. Because the broadband connection is so fast, the attraction data could be downloaded in real time to the kiosk. This is great because in the traditional kiosk where the attract loop is 30 or 60 seconds long, if a passing user sees it twice, he or she knows there isn't much to the kiosk. However, by making the kiosk a "front-end" delivery device and keeping all the content on a back-end server, you could continuously put new content into that server, thus keeping the kiosk fresh and updated. The old method required either physically going to the kiosk and changing the CD-ROMs it was running or disabling the unit and downloading a CD-ROM's amount of data via a dial-up line that in some cases took days. In addition, if you could somehow power your kiosk from solar energy and the consumer had a wireless connection, you could drop the content anywhere in the world.

Speaking of wireless, a lot of cool wireless devices are coming out that you should know about. First (in order of coolness), is the "Dick Tracy" cell phone wristwatch. Finally! Regardless of how viable this product is, or how comfortable it is, someone had to make it. The wristwatch can work two ways. In one mode it's like a speakerphone where you just hold your arm up and talk into it and listen. In the other mode you actually take the watch off and hold it up like a little cell phone. This cellular device has a lot of future potential. In its first incarnation, it is nothing more than a cell phone. However, like all current cell phones, it will move toward a Web-enabled format.

While the wireless cell phone market is just starting to take off in the United States, it has really hit in Europe and Japan. There, just like here, it seems everyone has a cell phone, except in Europe and Japan, all the cell phones come with Internet access. The trouble is, developers of websites and Internet services will need to see the protocols the device uses to connect with the Net. Most of these devices have very limited viewing screen size and almost none have color. The developer who wishes to target the cell phone wireless market will almost invariably have to develop two sites: one for normal views that enter with computers and one that is scaled and stripped down for the wireless market.

The wireless PDA market is something else that you might want to consider looking into. You will need to look at what you are offering and then decide if that is the market your business wishes to market to. Unfortunately, the current crop of PDAs with color screens have very small screens. They aren't as small as a cell phone screen, but they are no match for a 21-inch monitor. This means you could end up developing a version of your site for all these different devices, which would be laborious. Still, you might end up having to do this anyway, and the reward is that your customers could always reach you. If you plan on doing this, some general development advice is to develop your site for the computer market first. This version would offer the complete, 100 percent experience with graphics, sounds, video, and so forth. Then, as you encounter other distribution devices such as wireless PDAs and cell phones, you need only to copy your site and strip out those parts that are not compatible with that device's protocols.

Right now, the wireless market is only composed of PDAs and cell phones, because they are currently the only type of wireless devices available. In the future, however, the existence of a broad-band wireless network will seed the growth of a host of new wireless devices. For example, devices such as the e-book would do very well if wireless-enabled. The e-book is a device that is a little bigger than the Palm PDA but a little smaller than an 8.5 x 11-inch piece of paper. The device lets you connect to a book or magazine service provider and download material you like to read. It's back-lit and can flip orientation from horizontal to vertical and from a left-handed configuration to a right. You can also alter the size of the text, bookmark your pages, and so on. The current problem is that you need to connect the device to a computer to download the material that you want to read. Throw in a wireless connection and a few solar panels on its back cover, and the device could work from anywhere.

Wireless music is coming too. Devices such as the Rio and the Nomad allow you to play MP3s just like you used to play cassettes and CDs. In the future, as with the e-book, if these devices allow you to wirelessly connect to the Net, you won't have to download the music from a host computer. The advantage of this portable music-on-demand (we'll refer to it as pMOD) system is obvious. Just like a portable radio, this device will receive digital transmission of music like the MP3 and play it back. You could browse an onscreen LCD display of genres and song titles, then pick your song from a list of hundreds of thousands, or possibly even conduct searches for specific music tracks. The advantage of a device like this is that the music industry could still have some type of control by becoming a digital entertainment broadcasting megacomplex. Between songs the digital streams could be interjected with advertisements, announcements, and special concert information. Control would be put back into the hands of the labels, and customers would still get the convenience of listening to anything they wanted at any time. The pMOD device could become the radio of the future. Just like the analog cable offered 50 channels, then went digital and offered 500, the pMOD could replace the 50 or so radio stations by offering 500,000 stations to choose from.

The grand consumer-reaching device of them all is the wireless automobile. A lot of people are afraid of the Internet-enabled car because of a fear of the possibility of an increased number of accidents. However, this could be avoided by using voice-activated devices rather than screens. The advancements of digital signal processing (DSP) has made voice-activated devices more than an idea; they are in use today. AT&T uses voice-activated menus when you call for assistance. Some radio and CD manufacturers have already put voice-activated devices on the market, allowing you to change tracks by saying "Track 1" or "Track 2" to your stereo.

Traditionally, the trouble with voice-activated technology was the background noise. In an open office environment where everyone has voice-activated computers, it is almost impossible to get voice activation to work correctly. (We've heard of one person's travails when Apple computers put voice-activated commands into their OS. The person was working in an office that installed the voice-activated system. To get the computer's attention, you would say "computer." To get it to shut down, you would say "shut down."

Soon the users were opening applications and shutting down one another's computers at random. Needless to say, the system was soon disabled.)

The automobile has a host of electronic devices in it that already complement the coming broadband wireless wave. Cars have antennas, sound systems, navigation systems, and batteries. The sound system could be modified to include commands and responses from the Internet and could, in essence, read the site to you as you drove. You could visit specific sites that allow you to navigate them via voice command, similar to a Yahoo! search engine that is read to you, and you could make a voice selection to narrow your search. This would be how general searching and browsing could be accomplished, but other more specific functions such as communication and messaging would clearly be easy to develop with this type of system.

The car could be also outfitted with a navigation system that responded to a local information service. For example, the system could play a commercial of the restaurant you are approaching. Or, if you preprogrammed it with the kinds of places you like to eat, it could notify you that a new Japanese restaurant just opened up 1.5 miles from here, and ask you whether you would like directions.

UNDERSTANDING
THE FUTURE HOUSEHOLD

Thinking about tomorrow's world is not only fun, it can help you conceptualize new ways in which you can better enhance the broadband experience for your end user. Right now, most people are stuck thinking about the average consumer and their environment at present. Instead, think about them in terms of 5 and 10 years from now. This will give you a good model as to what to present to your future customers based on their lifestyle and experience.

While working on website projects for clients, we usually come up with user scenarios for what kinds of potential customers will be using the future site. We write up brief character analyses and stories that we can refer to as we work on the architecture and design of the site. This is a very helpful exercise because you can really start to discover what are the most important aspects of the site. As we work on navigation or design, we refer back to the characters in the user scenarios as a reference checking point, thinking, for example, "Okay, now that would work for Mary the executive, but Bob the schoolteacher will get lost."

To discover how people's everyday lives will change across the years because of the adoption broadband technologies, let's walk through two user scenarios that will cover a day in the life of a fictional family household. This will illustrate just how seamless technology will be in the home and the difference it will make in our lives. Of course, this isn't a literal prediction of what's going to happen, but it is somewhat based on the direction in which we are currently heading. So in the future, if you decide you are in a jam, you can refer back to these user scenarios or create your own.

FIVE YEARS AHEAD

It's a cold and rainy winter day in January 2005. Brad and Cathy are home on a Saturday with the kids because the weather is just too bad to go outside.

Billy is in Cathy's home office reciting his multiplication tables to the computer and checking his speed time. His classmate Tommy has a score that is higher than his. He has to beat it. He looks down at the other times in the class list and sees that Christina has a higher score as well. Suddenly a video message appears; it's Tommy making fun of his low score.

Melissa is practicing on the computerized piano. She enters in the song number from the book, and the monitor displays her previous progress on this beginning song. She pushes Start to let the piano autoplay so that she can hear the right tempo and the music, while watching the keys go up and down on the piano. She has it now. She presses another button to record and begins to play. The piano records her progress, cross-checking her performance with the correct way to play the song.

Brad is in the living room figuring out the new digital entertainment system he got a few days ago. Now with voice-activated commands, he can sit on the couch and say which movie he wants to see. He has set up the TV to program in his personal preferences. (No, he didn't care for Sandra Bullock, but he liked Meg Ryan.) Then he auto sets up the schedule by entering in channels created by some of his friends and coworkers in their spare time. He seems to enjoy their crazy broadcasts more than what is streaming in from the big networks, AtomFilms and AOL. Plus, he has everything linking right to his home network now that fiber optics are lined up in his neighborhood.

Cathy, on the other hand, is in the kitchen with the monitor that is handling the various home appliances. She sets up the washer to start the laundry at 2 P.M. so she wouldn't forget. The refrigerator reports that the family is running low on eggs, milk, and various other items and wants to confirm if the message can be sent to the grocery service as a placed order. Cathy confirms it, and the order is going to be delivered not only that day but within the hour.

TEN YEARS AHEAD

It's a mild summer day in July 2010. Brad and Cathy are now parents of one teenager (Billy is now 14) and one approaching her teens (Melissa is 12). With two young adults in the house, the couple is always faced with the fact that their kids are constantly distracted by movies, music, and shopping. But they are proud of how their kids have grown up and are learning so much.

Billy is in a basketball video community and is chatting in his room with John in Chicago about his favorite team. He shows him a video he edited and made from one of his high school basketball games. Amazed by the three pointer, John in Chicago comes back with his own video of a classic game at his school that won them the championships.

Melissa is away in Paris, France for summer school, but calls in on her portable video phone and is surfing the Web at the same time. Interrupting her brother's intense basketball conversation with John, she sends him some video footage of her in front of the Eiffel Tower and also gives him the web address for her latest work so that he can see what she is working on while she is away.

Meanwhile, Brad's in the garage in awe of his electric car. He was so excited when he finally got it that he couldn't sleep all night. He is waiting for Cathy to finish up her work in her home office so that they can go for a ride. The voice-activated door opens at his request and he steps inside and just stares at all the controls. The cars asks, "Where do you want to go? Please enter address." Brad laughs and says, "Nowhere just yet. Auto control, stop." Finally, Cathy comes into the garage, and the two drive off for a nice ride in the hills.

PROJECTING IS USEFUL

Whether or not the preceding scenarios actually take place, it's important to let your imagination go and start planning scenarios of how life can be as we integrate technology more seamlessly into our lives. Whatever models of industries we have now—television, Internet, commerce, and business—all the lines will blur and new definitions will start to form.

Although justifying each wild idea might be difficult and one might think it more prudent to follow safe and conventional modes of thought, it's not going to help you or your business in the long run. This period in the next five years will garner innovation and invention that will lay the foundation for the rest of the century. Be an early adopter and make sure that you are thinking far ahead enough to build a brand, company, or lifestyle that will inspire, empower, and illuminate everyday life.

THE CHANGING EMPLOYEE

You didn't think that the coming of a new technology such as broadband would be something that anyone could just understand, did you? With the introduction of this new type of high-speed communication comes a new type of employee, one who truly comprehends the technology involved. The broadband-capable employee knows a lot about programming languages that are relatively new. Languages such as JavaScript, Lingo, WAP, DHTML, Java, Jini, and Bluetooth all are excellent foundations to start with when looking for broadband programmers.

In the future, if you are not in e-business, you are going to be out of business. You have two choices. You can either implement e-business yourself or form a partnership with an agency that has a proven track record for setting up e-business companies. The partnership method requires nothing on your part except money and the faith that your partner will execute your vision.

If, however, you are going to brave e-business alone and build an internal team of employees to take on all the challenges a broadband world has to offer, you should know a little about what you are dealing with. Just as you have to begin to look at your company and its products or services differently now that broadband is a reality, your team must also be ready for the change. As their manager or executive, you will set the tone and pace of the environment you've created for them.

Many of the employees that can make this happen for your company are young, hip, and twice as smart as you. Everything that you know about computers they learned in grammar school and they have been learning more ever since. To this generation, computers are a second-nature tool that is as much a part of their lives as a pen is to yours. If computers confuse you, complicate your life, frustrate you, or generally make you feel intimidated, you need the younger generation of talent in your office that uses computers as easily as they tie their shoes.

Now don't feel bad if my last statements describe you, because what you have is the business savvy. This younger generation may be talented when it comes to computers, but you know what your business does and how it does it. You need to form a synergy together and create an e-presence for your company.

You should be aware of a few realities about hiring technical employees in this booming technical economy. One, they don't take any nonsense. They may not know your business, but they know the Internet and usually they know all the players and current pay rates, so keeping them can become a challenge. If you have an office with no windows, where everyone is required to wear ties or dress up and (God forbid) you have cubicles, you are going to have a hard time attracting these employees, let alone keeping them for more than six months. The environment this type of employee works in is very important. These employees know that technically their "work" is done on a computer that is connected to the Internet and therefore could be done from anywhere in the world. Why should they do it in a 6 x 9-foot cubical in the back corner of an office with no window when they could be writing code with a PowerBook wirelessly connected to the network on a train bound for Paris? They will be more productive workers when you give them freedom and deadlines. Putting up with their skateboarding to work, tattoos, and orange-colored hair is worth it because what you hopefully get in return is two dollars back for every one spent in e-business.

Because of the dot com revolution, people with Internet engineering skills and multimedia engineering skills are in high demand. If, however, you need these type of employees and you expect their introduction into your existing office environment will be too disruptive, set up a virtual private LAN (VPN) and let them connect in from home or anywhere else.

Something to consider as well is your current staff of employees. Do they need to change to understand and adopt this broadband "attitude" in order for your business to be successful too? Yes, they do. You will find that once your company starts doing e-commerce business, it could become a substantial part of your company's revenue. You might end up with a staff of employees who don't really know what your company does anymore. This can eventually lead to attrition.

In order to help your employees adapt to the coming broadband economy, you need to start introducing them to the technology in a fashion that presents it as a way of saving time and money. This in turn should help foster an inquisitive nature in them and help them make the transition to acceptance. PDAs, cell phones, laptop computers, and free Internet home access for the employees might be a good way to start. Not only will they become more acquainted with the technology, they will be rewarded with perks for their efforts.

THE BROADBAND EMPLOYEE AND DIRECTION

Following are a few steps you can take in building a successful and efficient broadband team:

1. Decide whether to partner or not.

2. Find specialized programmers from recruiters.

3. Build an internal team.

4. Craft a vision that meets your business.

5. Let that team create the vision and learn.

What type of people do you need for your broadband teams? Your business is your business, but e-business (and broadband in particular) involves a specific type of employee with the certain job description. A lot of different levels of engineers and other resources with various technical skill sets are needed to form a really effective team and you will need to prepare your company for its entry into the broadband world. The first skill set is HTML programming. Obviously, you will need at least one HTML person, if not several. Next up is JavaScript. Keep in mind that JavaScript is not Java. For those readers who do not know, JavaScript is a programming language that sits inside the HTML code and allows web browsers to become more interactive. Rolling over a picture could reveal yet another picture, for example. Generally, HTML and JavaScript are so tightly written that you shouldn't have problems finding an engineer who knows both languages.

From here you enter into the programming languages that start costing more, and the people who know the skills get a bit harder to find. Languages such as Java, ASP, Perl, CGI, WebObjects, PHP, and Lingo are all excellent tools to have in your staff arsenal. Java, for example, will allow the creation of interactive web experiences that don't require any plug-ins to deliver them. It can also compile the experience into a standalone application that can be delivered on any platform. ASP, CGI, WebObjects, PHP, and Perl are back-end server-side programming languages that are all at the forefront of e-commerce.

The next type of person you will need is someone that is a visionary—someone who can separate the forest from the trees, so to speak. (This may be you.) This type of person knows the business of e-commerce really well and is intimately familiar with the tools that power e-commerce. This doesn't mean that the person will be a programmer—he or she will be more like the director of Internet technologies or the director of research and development. This person should, however, work with your CTO (chief technology officer) on a regular basis to make sure that the needs of the company match the needs your client is demanding.

CASE STUDY

ReplayTV

Interactive television meets broadband

www.replaytv.com

Television is not a luxury these days; most people cannot live without it. For most U.S. households, the TV is a staple in the home. As TV viewers, we follow the characters in our favorite shows faithfully, as if they were our own friends, and the shows frequently serve as topics of conversation with our own friends and acquaintances. When television first came on the scene back in the 1950s, no one could have predicted the giant industry it was about to create. Fast-forward 50 years later, and television is about to redefine itself once again, this time for the broadband generation. ReplayTV, a Silicon Valley–based company, is banking on the fact that television is the medium that will fuel broadband's acceptance by the masses. After all, consumers have TVs at home already and cable modems have an early lead in the broadband market.

ReplayTV is the personal television service and digital recorder that captures TV shows. The ReplayTV product is essentially a hard drive with a modem connected to the television. But don't call it a VCR. All TV shows are recorded digitally and stored onto the hard drive, which can hold up to 20 hours. Because it all works digitally, things don't need to work linearly. Don't want to miss a Julia Roberts or Tom Cruise movie? No problem. Set up your ReplayTV so that your favorite actors, actresses, movies, sport teams, or even hobbies can always be recorded, without you having to know what's on the TV schedule. It's your own personal TV, 24 hours a day.

But think about this. You're watching *Frasier*, and the phone rings. Push Pause, and the show will wait for you—a TV lover's dream. ReplayTV breaks down the time barrier even while watching live TV. Users can pause during a show at anytime, go back, or view things in slow motion. A 30-second QuickScan button allows you to quickly skip those pesky commercials. It's like being in a time warp!

Revolutionizing the concept of television is only part of what ReplayTV is doing. "We are looking forward to the day when Broadband takes off because it will enable so many new services for us," says Steve Shannon, vice president of marketing for ReplayTV. "Imagine being able to integrate a movie trailer into our on-screen Showtime guide. There are dozens of great things we could do like that once that bandwidth is there."

And ReplayTV is relying on the fact that high-bandwidth will be the way of the future. Already backed by such top new media players as Paul Allen and venture capital firm Kleiner Perkins Caufield & Byers, ReplayTV is setting the course to create the standards and implement innovative technology in order to rise to the top in this new marketplace. And how does ReplayTV create a broadband vision? By continually researching the trends in technology that will further the company's vision of television in the future. By watching the ways in which media, cable, and the Internet industry move, ReplayTV is better positioned to find the means to converge these existing and evolving industries with that of television.

As both a hardware and service company, ReplayTV is also changing the notion of how businesses are being defined in this fresh new arena. Merging new technology with service, ReplayTV unveiled its ReplayZones at the beginning of 2000. The ReplayZones are a content-rich "portal for television" that will give subscribers to ReplayTV new ways to find and record their TV shows. ReplayZones include destinations like Movie Zone, Sitcoms, Westerns, Talk Show Guests, Replay Picks, Search, and Create a Theme. Users can select a category and get a list of upcoming shows in a format that's targeted to their interests. Then all they have to do is push a button to have their favorites recorded.

Hmmm. . . Broadband and content. Sound familiar? This is only the beginning. ReplayTV hopes that major media partners will want to get in on the action and have special sponsored zones where they can highlight specific programs for promotions. Showtime and NBC have already lined up their own channel, and it will only be a matter of time before the other networks and cable channels follow suit. These sponsored channels will allow networks the ability to advertise upcoming shows and tie in to specific promotions.

With other potential companies entering this interactive television/service market and with prime competitors like TiVO, it will be interesting to see just how far ReplayTV and its ReplayTV Service will redefine the way in which consumers think about television, content, and personalization as it plays a major role in the future of broadband.

CHAPTER 10

Final Thoughts
on
Reaching the Last Mile

W e know you want to hear our final prediction for the future. Here it is: The future world will be just like the cartoon *The Jetsons*. Yes, that's right. You'll be flying around in tiny saucers, have robots as servants, and shuffle around on moving conveyer belts. Just watch and see.

Okay, we were kidding. However, we do hope that this book has enlightened you about broadband's possibilities. We want you to come away with the ability to understand the foundation for the technology, as well as the critical thinking necessary to comprehend all the complex merging, acquiring, innovation, and movement companies are making. This is your chance to be an early adopter in this new realm. Looking back on the Internet, we're sure most people could kick themselves for not seeing it all sooner—for not writing that Internet business plan back in 1994 or 1995 because they were too tired and for not investing in stocks such as Yahoo! or Netscape. We've been there, and we're looking out for you now.

WE ARE ONLY HUMAN

Here's our spiritual part of the book as it relates to technology. Humans are made up of two parts, a body and a mind. The mind is what we use to fabricate our vision, and the body delivers that vision. The connection of mind to mind is where the broadband revolution is taking us. We have five senses, and the computer can currently transmit vision and hearing effectively. Smelling devices for the computer are already on the way. The direction technology is going leads to the creation of a true full sensory transmission device—a device that has an enormous cache stored inside the middle to store the information that is passing through it. (Is this starting to sound like virtual reality?)

We as individuals need to have a communication device that can handle a few things that we physically can't, such as transmission at the speed of light. Those tiny electrons and photons moving through wires and fiber today are already traveling that fast. The bottleneck is simply the interface between the computer and human. We have the need to be able to contact anyone at anytime. We need information at the speed of light.

Once we are all wired or wirelessly connected, human evolution has the potential to change dramatically. Cultural, economical barriers, and racial barriers will have the potential to be diminished. Computers will be able to translate any language into any other language in real time, making conversations with foreigners not foreign at all. People will be able to share ideas without the barriers of status, age, or gender getting in the way. When information, ideas, and communication take place in an open forum such as the Internet, we are all equal regardless of age, size, color, geography, gender, or any other difference we may have.

In some ways our natural progression to broadband stems out of the mentality that we are always trying to do things faster and save time. Yet the catch-22 is that the more devices and technological enhancement used to essentially save time, the busier we all become. But our quest for newer, faster, better and the desire for knowledge are what broadband is really seeded from. If someone asks you "Do you know why the sky is blue?" and you don't know the answer, he or she will simply go elsewhere to seek it out. It's a part of human nature. Because of this, broadband is the next natural progression toward the human race being able to solve problems faster, to communicate with one another quicker, and to be instantly entertained when it wants to be.

THE OOH, AH PHASE

Right now, everything related to broadband is being hyped. The Time Warner/AOL merger has just made it worse. Confusion abounds as businesses are asking themselves what does this merger mean? and what will this convergence bring us? Whether or not these sites or hybrid companies are producing anything doesn't matter. The news media eats it up and disseminates it to the rest of us, including those at the top of companies. It will almost be like the first days of the Internet when graphic design hardly mattered and a web presence was all you needed. But don't fall into that trap because it won't be in this stage for long. To be successful in the coming broadband marketplace, we suggest you partner up with a content provider, or better yet, experts in film, video, or motion graphics. They will know how elements should move, and if they have a background in the Web, they'll also understand interactivity and personalization.

The current crop of web professionals are stuck in the "design for now" stage. Make sure people you are working with are visionaries like you. Here's where we can use the expertise of all those CD-ROM developers from a while back. Impress them all with your broadband vision and strategy. Think it through. Test it.

Experiment. Then develop it. If you build yourself a strong foundation, you'll find that you'll have a stronger "house" in the long run. In short, make sure you have a broadband strategy that will not only put you at the forefront of your industry, but that will have the right foundation for longevity.

This technology has the potential to set us free. Using wireless devices to stay connected to other coworkers at work as well as to your friends, to your family, and the vast Internet repository of knowledge and services will be a natural part of our everyday lives. If done correctly, the wireless device will be generic enough to allow anyone to log in (like a computer) and use others' wireless devices. Cars of the future will have wireless information systems that are voice-controlled and offer you navigation, entertainment, and assistance in time of trouble. These same systems will allow you to communicate with anyone in the world, even someone on the moon. (Okay, that might be reaching a bit, but if someone dreams about it, it's bound to happen!)

FORECASTING AHEAD

In short, we understand that you want to know what to expect in the future, and for the most part, that's what this whole book has been about: helping you get a grasp for the new technology that is right on our horizon. So just what is on the horizon exactly?

Here are our top 10 predictions for the future in the next few years. These are in no particular order of importance, because quite frankly, all of them are important in the broadband revolution.

1. *Smart devices will be a part of our daily lives.* The ability for technology to be integrated seamlessly into your business world as well as the everyday world will happen with smart devices. These will first be adopted through

hand-held devices and cell phones, and later in appliances such as refrigerators and washers/dryers.

2. *Video-on-demand and interactive TV will be commonplace.* Movies will become downloadable digital goods that will be available via download to your TV, moving the video rental market from its current physical space to the online world. Interactive TV will change the way TV programming and advertising is handled. Users will watch what they want, when they want.

3. *DSL will triumph over cable.* DSL technology will win out over the cable industry as consumers realize the limitations of cable—more importantly, the bad cable infrastructure where users are sharing cable bandwidth with their neighbors.

4. *Broadband sites will multiply.* We'll see an increase of sites that use full interactive video, audio, and pictures. Sites will move away from heavy text and reading of content, to more engaging visual, narrative experiences.

5. *Video conferencing over the Internet will take off.* From every office boardroom to the average home-office, everyone will be better equipped to have video conference meetings or phone calls with crisp, clear, technology. Broadcast through the Internet, video conferencing of the future will give today's jumpy webcams a run for their money.

6. *Cars will be equipped with Internet access.* With wireless technology, all new cars will be equipped with a computer that has wireless access to the Internet.

7. *The music industry will move to digital goods.* Your old CD's, not to mention your old records and tapes, will become collectors items as MP3 technology starts the emergence of the buying and selling of music for download online.

8. *Energy companies will become major players in the Internet.* Already, one company has figured out a way to send the Internet data through the electro-magnetic field that surrounds the power line. Others will follow as they try to find new ways to bring broadband to the masses.

9. *Wireless Internet utilization will increase at significant rate.* Wireless access will increase because of the widespread use of smart devices as well as wireless access through cars.

10. *Fiber optics will be deployed to the home in the next three to five years.* Fiber-optic lines are being laid out across all major cities today and we will finally see some adoption to homes. The last mile will be reached!

Congratulations! You've successfully absorbed the world of broadband. But don't stop here. Keep on reading or watching the latest technology news. Ask your co-workers what they think of certain topics or companies. Fuel the discourse. Visit our website too (www.lastmilebook.com) as an online resource to this book, which is filled with links that can help you in your research on creating the best broadband strategy for your company.

Most of all, don't give up! We haven't. We are here to support you. And although you may run into a few naysayers along the way, don't let their pessimism dampen your view on the potential for the future. This is a radical departure from the current state of the Internet, but it is the ultimate expansion of the use of a high-speed communication network that will allow us humans to connect with one another.

Be an innovator and bring broadband to your business, because when the last mile is reached, you'll be way ahead of the competition.

TOP TEN REASONS
TO DREAD "SMART" APPLIANCES

1. *Over the Limit* The bathroom scale keeps telling the fridge to stop ordering food.

2. *Tattle Snooze* Your smart pillow talks to your PC, which emails your boss with a message that, yep, you've overslept again.

3. *Brand Name* Not only does your stovetop grill know when steak is cooked to your exact specifications, but it sears a nice flying Windows logo onto each side.

4. *Buying on Spec* Sunglasses combine UV protection with real-time stock quotes, but laugh maniacally when you approach margin calls.

5. *Car Talk* Your dashboard computer insists on making blonde jokes about your driving.

6. *Rotten Sense of Humor* The perky "kitchen assistant," an animated onscreen spatula, keeps calling your mobile phone and asking, "Is your refrigerator running?"

7. *Lack of Privacy* Your mailbox keeps asking why you get so many plain brown packages.

8. *No Dim Bulbs* Your lamps are so full of bright ideas you have to pay for their MENSA memberships.

9. *High Maintenance* Your appliances secretly open a joint bank account for repair-person kickbacks.

10. *Anticompetitive Practices* Your Microsoft coffeemaker monopolizes the countertop.

(Reprinted from CNET Digital Dispatch April 28, 2000, written by Steve Fox, Michael Leverton, and Heather Brossard, www.cnet.com, with permission from CNET, Inc., copyright ©1995-2000.)

Glossary

ABR

Available bit rate; refers to the bandwidth of an ATM **broad-**band transmission.

ATM

Asynchronous Transfer Mode; the method by which **data** is sent via a broadband network.

BBS

Bulletin board system; an electronic communication **server** that allows messages to be posted from multiple users.

Bluetooth

A technology that links devices together using wireless communication protocols.

brick and mortar

Used to define and differentiate physical stores from **online** e-commerce shops.

business-to-business e-commerce (B-to-B)

The selling of goods or services online between companies, usually at competitive bulk prices.

business-to-consumer e-commerce (B-to-C)

The selling of goods or services online between a company and the general public.

CBR

Constant bit rate; refers to how data flows through an ATM network.

cable modem

A device that blends the normal cable box with a computer modem, giving you both features in one device.

consumer-to-consumer e-commerce (C-to-C)

The selling of goods or services online between individuals of the general public. Transactions are usually done through auction sites like eBay or Amazon.com.

DSL

Digital Subscriber Line; the conversion of an analog phone signal to a digital signal.

e-commerce

Electronic commerce; the buying and selling of goods and services online.

extranet

A private website shared by multiple companies and clients to collaborate on projects or share work.

fiber optics

Cables made of fiber that pass light and are used to transmit data.

flash

A vector-based application that allows the animation of vector artwork over time. The animation can be played back over the Internet.

GPS

Global positioning system; a system of satellites that surrounds the earth, broadcasting a signal that is used by devices on Earth to triangulate the exact position of the devices.

HAVi

Home Audio/Video interoperability; a series of connection cables and software that allows devices to communicate with one another.

HLT

Home Linking Technology; the connection and communication of devices via the existing electrical power in the home.

interactive TV

> Promised to be the "future of television," interactive TV merges the interactivity of the Web with the functionality of today's TV to connect users directly to content.

Jini

> A programming language that can be run on any device, such as a cell phone, PDA, home appliance, and so on.

intranet

> A private internal network within a company firewall that is not accessible to the public.

LMDS

> Local multipoint distribution service; a fixed wireless two-way broadband distribution system.

MP3

> Digital audio format that allows for high CD quality audio and streaming capabilities.

MPEG

> Motion Picture Experts Group; the MPEG file is the delivery format for compressed high-quality video.

nrt-VBR

> Non-real-time variable bit rate; refers to the bandwidth of an ATM broadband transmission.

PDA

> Personal digital assistant; the PALM is a PDA.

QuickTime

> Technical architecture in the form of software that allows video to enter a computer and be played back.

rt-VBR

> Real-time variable bit rate; refers to the bandwidth of an ATM broadband transmission.

rich media

> Interactive content on the Web that goes beyond ordinary HTML web pages, such as animation, video, and audio capabilities.

Shockwave

The delivery technology used to stream both Flash and Director movies that allows its playback in a web browser.

splitter

A device that separates and routes the Internet data to your computer and the phone data to your phone; used with DSL.

throughput

The amount of data that can travel through a medium (such as wires). Throughput can also be used to describe a device that data travels through, for example, a 56-kbps modem has an effective throughput of 4 kbps.

UBR

Unspecified bit rate; refers to the bandwidth of an ATM broad-band transmission.

UPNP

Universal plug-and-play; devices and software that allow a connection through the already-existing standard Internet protocols.

video-on-demand

The ability of consumers to digitally download movies or content to view anytime.

VOXML

Voice-Activated Markup Language; a programming language that allows the user to speak via phone to a web page.

Index

ABOUT THE AUTHORS

Jason Wolf is Director of Multimedia/Internet Technology and Regional Director of Research and Development at marchFIRST in San Francisco, CA (formerly USWeb/CKS). An acknowledged thought leader in the area of collaborative unification of traditional multimedia and Internet technologies, he has developed landmark Internet marketing initiatives and multimedia projects for Nike, Apple, Levi's, Visa, Transamerica, GM, MCI, Pixar, and other Fortune 100 clients. Prior to joining marchFIRST, he worked for Macromedia, where he helped develop Shockwave.

Natalie Zee is an Interactive Design Director and co-founder of the Research and Development Department at marchFIRST in San Francisco, CA (formerly USWeb/CKS). As an award-winning designer, she leads interactive Web projects for such clients as Apple, Levi's, Visa, Harman Kardon, and other prominent companies. Prior to joining marchFIRST, she was a Web Designer at Macromedia, launching both macromedia.com, one of the top ten Web sites, and Shockwave, the leading interactive component on the Web today Zee has also worked as a designer at Frogdesign, working with clients such as Bank of America, CommerceOne, and SAP. She holds a degree in Mass Communications and Technology from U.C. Berkeley. Natalie Zee is also the author of the bestselling Web design books, *HTML Artistry: More than Code* and *HTML Web Magic*.

DATE DUE

GAYLORD			PRINTED IN U.S.A.